MAKING IT WORK AT HOME

MAKING IT WORK AT HOME

A PRACTICAL GUIDE TO WORKING FROM HOME

ANNA WRIGHT

This edition first published in Great Britain 2008 by
Crimson Publishing, a division of Crimson Business Ltd
Westminster House
Kew Road
Richmond
Surrey
TW9 2ND

A catalogue record for this book is available from the British library.

ISBN 978 1 85458 438 0
Exclusive Brother edition: 978 1 85458 451 9 (not available through trade)

Printed and bound by Mega Printing, Turkey

Contents

Taking the big leap

1

Where do you work? Even if the official answer is 'the office', chances are that you take business calls while on the train or in your car, read reports in cafés, and catch up with admin in front of the television at night. If you have never checked your emails between courses at a restaurant or headed for the hotel pool armed with a towel and your laptop, undoubtedly you will have caught others in the act. The concept of the nine-to-five job is fast becoming extinct, consigned with office tea trolleys, handwritten memos and full-size editions of *The Times* to another era.

In the 21st century, office work is tied not to an individual desk or hard drive but to the person doing it. By 2013, experts predict that fewer than half of the office-working population will routinely set out for their desks in the morning. Statistically, you will be more likely to finish your breakfast and head upstairs to what was the spare room, or down the garden to your purpose-built Wi-Fi shed.

So if you're planning to take the plunge now, you are ahead of the game but – whatever the reaction of your boss, colleagues and others – far from being a pioneer. Twenty years ago, in most occupations the very idea of homeworking was almost unthinkable. Fifteen years ago, it was seen largely as the preserve of the teenagers building the dotcom phenomenon from their bedrooms. But by the late 1990s, the home office was becoming a common feature in the houses of high-ranking professionals in particular – although they were used principally during evenings and weekends, as an addition rather than as an alternative to the daily workplace. Currently, a

conservative estimate places homeworkers at around 12.5% of the overall workforce – that's one in eight, a figure that has more than doubled in a decade. The pace of change is such that statistics on the subject are out of date by the time they have been collated.

The real numbers of homeworkers are almost certainly much higher. Estimates such as the above are based on national statistics that take into consideration only those people who work mainly in their own home or use it as a base for their work. The majority of teleworkers, who work from home for one or two days a week or on a more occasional basis are therefore excluded. The government figures also ignore the increasing numbers of people who work from within the grounds or structure of their home, but not technically within their home itself. So none of those labouring away in converted garages, annexes or garden offices are included in the final tally.

>Who works from home?

According to the statistics the average UK homeworker is a middle-aged man of some professional weight. He is quite likely to be self-employed – at present more than four in 10 teleworkers are – but if he is an employee then he will be one with enough seniority to influence his own working hours and set-up. However, the homeworking demographic is changing as rapidly as the numbers themselves. The practice is increasing in popularity not only among the managerial ranks and self-employed high-fliers, but also among people working in human resources (HR), marketing, administrative, sales, services and other roles, as well as those, such as stay-at-home mums, who were previously not working through circumstance rather than choice.

> **Definition:**
>
> **Teleworking:**
> Working from home or another location, specifically using communication technology such as phone, email, video conferencing and private networks to maintain contact with colleagues and clients.

Homeworking is currently most common – and growing fastest – among the older age groups. It is estimated that 18% of the over-50s are teleworkers – due, in part, to part-time or flexible working patterns and the lack of a commute encouraging an extended working life. The primary reason, however, is the lingering notion that career status earns someone the right to work from home, at least some of the time. This attitude is also partly responsible for the fact that around only 15% of workers aged 35–49 and 4% of those aged 16–24 telework. It is also backed by anecdotal evidence from employees who feel that they aren't trusted to work from home, despite it being common practice among their superiors.

The divide is even more marked among the occasional teleworkers, where managers and senior officials make up 37% of the total, professionals another 37%, and

Top occupations for teleworking:

① =Managers and senior officials	23
① =Associate professional and technical	23
③ Professional occupations	18
④ Skilled trades occupations	17
⑤ Administrative and secretarial	10
⑥ Personal service occupations	4
⑦ Sales and customer service occupations	2
⑧ Process plant and machine operatives	2
⑨ Elementary occupations	1

associate professional and technical occupations 17% – an overwhelming 91% between them.

Already, though, attitudes in companies are changing and the boundaries are coming down, with responses to homeworking requests less inclined to be a blanket no and more likely to take account of individual experience, suitability and job requirements. This has been steered by government guidelines encouraging greater work–life balance for employees, spearheaded by legislation giving a statutory right to apply for flexible working to almost anyone with a young or disabled child or a partner or relative for whom they act as a carer. But it is mostly driven by a substantial shift in outlook from the private sector. The old viewpoint was that while the public sector might be able to pamper staff with work–life balance and wellbeing initiatives, private companies fighting for survival in the real world simply couldn't afford to be so nice. Yet, as homeworking has become more popular and the consequences clearer, some major private corporations and smaller enterprises have recognised that the benefits of homeworking will be seen in their profits too.

> **Definition:**
>
> **Flexiworking, flexible working**
> Any work pattern adapted to meet individual needs, whether working from home, job sharing, or working part-time, at unusual times, for more hours over fewer days (compressed) or fluctuating hours over the year to accommodate school holidays or similar (annualised).

One knock-on effect has been the introduction of homeworking into occupations that have not in the past looked for alternatives to a central office. The virtual call centres set up by some large UK companies are a case in point: a customer services representative could now just as feasibly be picking up the phone in their own spare room as in one of the large open-plan offices. It is expected to take off particularly in areas such as sales, which have traditionally required a great deal of travel that could be largely eliminated if employees were more strategically located.

>Role of the technology revolution

It is, of course, no coincidence that the trend for homeworking has developed alongside the rise of mobile phones, the spread of broadband internet and the plummeting price and size of basic office technology.

In the latest government survey, nearly 90% of teleworkers declared they could not work from home without both a telephone and a computer. More than 99% of homes and businesses in the UK can now have broadband, and though the much-discussed blanket Wi-Fi coverage of major cities has yet to materialise on a large scale, wireless internet is increasingly available, from coffee shops and leisure centres to train carriages. As laptops get slimmer and lighter, hand-held devices ever more sophisticated and third-generation (3G) mobile technology more prevalent, communication in a living room, café or literally on the move is equal in speed and quality to that provided in a corporate set-up.

At the same time, the growing affordability of high-calibre printers and proliferation of space-saving multifunction devices on the market, has brought home offices right up to par. Technology such as Voice over Internet Protocol (VoIP) and cheap deals on joint phone and internet connections as the competition between providers hots up, are also a significant factor in making running a business from home financially viable. With most of the major office-product manufacturers and dealers launching more and larger SoHo (small office/home office) lines and keen to push this side of their business, the choice and efficiency of products tailored specifically to the homeworker is only going to increase.

>Why escape the office?

As discussed above, advances in technology have provided the means – and increasingly office equipment is being developed with the home market firmly in mind – but the motivation lies elsewhere. Surveys consistently put commuting and work itself at the bottom of the list when it comes to lifestyle satisfaction. The UK has the longest working hours in Europe. It is the only country in the European Union that allows employees to opt out of the average 48-hour limit laid down in the working time regulations, and the existing laws aren't routinely enforced. One in six people now put in more than 60 hours a week, and the numbers are increasing. Almost five million people regularly do unpaid overtime, working nearly two months of every year for free, effectively donating an average £5,000 to their employers in the process. Add to that the fact that a typical London commuter now spends a whole month of each year travelling to and from work (it's a still-alarming 139 hours elsewhere in the country) and it's little surprise that so many people are looking for an alternative way of working.

In recent years, perfect work–life balance has become the Holy Grail. The search has been fuelled by an increasing awareness of the health implications and other negative effects of a high-stress, 24/7 working environment. But for many people, it becomes a kind of vicious circle. They move out into the countryside or to the coast in the hope of a more relaxed pace of life, only to find they are spending hours every morning and evening in a traffic jam or stuck on a delayed and crowded train. Between the 1990s and the present decade, the number of people facing a commute of more than 50km (31 miles) increased by 30%. Commuting long distances by car has been linked to physical problems, including lower back and neck pain, tiredness, high blood pressure and tension, as well as anger and irritability and a diminished ability to perform some tasks. Workers who put in long hours of overtime are also over 60% more likely to fall ill or to be injured. The immediate consequences of these work patterns are compounded by the fact that extended periods travelling and sitting at a desk, leaving little opportunity – or energy – for exercise, visits to the doctor or socialising. They have also contributed in a major way to the increasing consumption of fat and caffeine-laden snacks and meals on the go.

Any idea that as a homeworker you will begin every morning with a wholesome bowl of cereal, kick the cappuccino habit and shut down your computer with a satisfied sigh at 5pm on the dot each evening will probably disappear with your first deadline. However, homeworkers are healthier. At least, they take significantly fewer sick days, and that's a huge advantage for the employee, employer and

tax-payer alike. Staff absence costs the UK economy upwards of £13.4 billion (or 175 million working days) a year. In some jobs, the cost of a single worker's annual sick leave can be more than £1,200, and that's a burden few small businesses can carry.

Several possible factors make working from home better for you than office life. Greater flexibility in your working hours, even if the total number of hours remains the same or increases, can give you an opportunity for exercise when you feel most energetic or when a playing partner is available, or just for short pick-me-ups throughout the day, whether it's a brisk walk round the block or stomach crunches on the bedroom floor. A well-stocked fridge and cupboards also remove the need – or lessen the temptation – for a fast-food lunch and a mid-afternoon trip to the coffee shop for the obligatory round of lattes and muffins.

>Employer benefits

A recent survey revealed that, whatever the health problem, two out of three people can and are willing to work from home on days they phone in sick. So it is the commute or the danger of infecting colleagues that is probably keeping them from their desks. Of course, a certain proportion of absentees on any given day will

Reasons to work at home:

- Waving goodbye to a stuffy, air-conditioned environment with sometimes large numbers of people, and their colds and other allergies, in close proximity

- Moving out of a tense, high-pressure atmosphere. One in four people take sick leave due to stress, costing the UK economy around £1.25 billion a year

- Cutting down on the time you spend battling with public transport and other road-users

- Flexible working hours

- Saving money that would have gone on take away coffees and treats

simply be throwing a sickie. Employers believe 12% of sick days are taken on false pretences, with 70% saying staff extend their weekends, 68% saying there is a clear connection between sickies and holidays, and 39% making a link between supposed illness and major events such as sports tournaments. The last assumption is backed by four in 10 football fans having admitted lying to get the day off during the World Cup. So whether because homeworkers are more motivated by their working lives in general or keen to prove to sceptical bosses that being out of sight doesn't mean slacking off (or, in fact, because they are keeping one eye on the big match on television), they are apparently far less likely to fake illness.

More relaxed, inspired workers are not only less susceptible to poor health, but measurably more productive. Although the public sector led the way with flexible-working policies, private companies have rapidly caught on to the potential benefits to their bottom line. More than 10% of BT's 100,000 employees are home based, with 70% working flexibly in terms of hours and location. As a result, BT has experienced a 63% drop in sick leave and a 20% increase in productivity. Analysis by the AA, which runs a virtual call centre alongside its more traditional operation, with homeworkers answering the phones, also showed a rise in productivity of between 10% and 40%.

In addition, BT has made savings of over £350 million in office overheads. According to analysts, the average small business can generate efficiency gains of at least 20% in the same way. Encouraging homeworking makes the recruitment process considerably easier, giving companies access to a greater pool of candidates and allowing them to select entirely on the basis of skills and suitability, once geographical proximity has been taken out of the equation.

BT has also been hugely successful in holding onto valued female employees after they have had children. Offering the option of homeworking to fit in around childcare and school runs has boosted the company's maternity retention rate to 99%, compared with a national average of just 47 %. This approach not only cuts business costs in recruitment and training, but also increases a company's appeal as an employer to the huge numbers of women finding it all but impossible to combine career and motherhood. According to one recent survey, although flexibility is the top priority for the majority of mothers when searching for jobs, 83 % have problems finding flexible work that actually uses their skills. Over two-thirds of those currently unemployed want to work but don't see why they should settle for jobs considerably below their level of skill and experience just to get the flexibility they need.

>The gender gap

Well-qualified mothers embracing homeworking as a route back into work is a major growth area – and one that is redressing the current imbalance between the sexes.

The global story

In terms of sheer numbers, the USA leads the world in teleworking, more commonly known as telecommuting outside Europe. A recent survey found that 23 % of US workers regularly work from a location outside the office, and analysts expect the total tally to approach one billion by 2011 (although the criteria are more encompassing than in equivalent UK studies). Proportionately, Canada and Australia are almost keeping pace with the USA, possibly driven by some of the lowest internet costs in the world and the long commutes created by low population densities spread over large areas.

In Europe, UK and Germany boast almost half of all teleworkers in absolute numbers, followed by the Netherlands, Italy, France and Sweden. In terms of proportions however, the picture is very different. The countries with the highest proportion of teleworkers in the total population are Finland, Sweden, the Netherlands, Denmark and Switzerland, followed by the UK. Spain, France and Italy sit at the bottom of the league, though teleworking is currently increasing most rapidly in Germany and Italy. Europe-wide, 75 % of teleworkers are men, and half of all home-based teleworking women have children under six.

Historically, the UK was fastest on the uptake, with 5.4 % of the workforce doing some kind of telework in the early 1990s way ahead of the rest of the EU, which held onto its traditional manufacturing strength for longer. During the 1980s the negative image of teleworking was such that the trade unions almost universally condemned it as exploitative, and in both Germany and the USA, there were proposals to legally ban the practice.

The latest government figures show that men make up 67 % of the total telework force, compared with a far more even 53 % of the workforce as a whole. This is tied in to the preponderance of men in the managerial, professional and technical roles that currently dominate teleworking. The increasing number of female managers in the overall workplace will have an impact, as will the spread of the homeworking trend into more traditionally female occupations, including human resources and training, where improving work–life balance remains a hot topic.

Ironically, the old-style, non-technology-based form of homeworking was overwhelmingly female. Typically poorly paid and requiring little in the way of education or qualifications, this has largely been

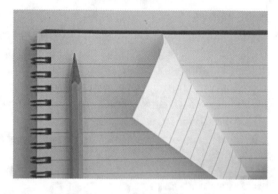

stamped out as women have found more profitable, challenging and worthwhile ways of combining work with motherhood.

>The homeworking map of the UK

The geographical spread of homeworking is spearheaded by the south-east of England, again with a high density of (mainly male) management professionals, but emerging from behind that is a different pattern. Those living in remote locations have traditionally, like many working mothers, had to downsize their aspirations and their salaries to meet their circumstances. The Dick Whittington effect is very much alive and well for graduates, in particular. The belief persists that the jobs are in London (and, to a lesser extent, Manchester and Edinburgh and the UK's other major cities). If you move beyond the commuter belt, you can no longer expect to work at the cutting edge of your profession or earn the kind of money your urban contemporaries are taking home. Undeniably, in some industries and certain companies, whether because of a genuine necessity to be close to the action or simply an entrenched culture, that is still the case. However, successful businesses have been set up in remote areas of the British Isles, and in some cases are providing local employment opportunities in communities where the lack of work is a growing problem, showing that homeworking can be more than a lifestyle choice. As the proportionate figures indicate, in some of the UK's poorest and most isolated regions, these businesses are an economic lifeline.

Nearly 12% of the rural workforce operates from home, compared with 8% in urban areas, and the figures in the countryside are swelled by a higher than

<table>
<tr><td colspan="2">Top UK regions for homeworking:</td></tr>
<tr><td>By percentage of workforce</td><td>By total numbers</td></tr>
<tr><td>① South East</td><td>① South East</td></tr>
<tr><td>② South West</td><td>② London</td></tr>
<tr><td>③ =East</td><td>③ East</td></tr>
<tr><td>③ =London</td><td>④ South West</td></tr>
<tr><td>⑤ East Midlands</td><td>⑤ North West</td></tr>
<tr><td>⑥ =Wales</td><td>⑥ West Midlands</td></tr>
<tr><td>⑥ =West Midlands</td><td>⑦ East Midlands</td></tr>
<tr><td>⑧ =North West</td><td>⑧ Yorkshire and Humberside</td></tr>
<tr><td>⑧ =Yorkshire and Humberside</td><td>⑨ Scotland</td></tr>
<tr><td>⑩ =North East</td><td>⑩ Wales</td></tr>
<tr><td>⑪ =Scotland</td><td>⑪ North East</td></tr>
<tr><td>⑫ Northern Ireland</td><td>⑫ Northern Ireland</td></tr>
</table>

average percentage of self-employed workers, freelancers and small-business owners. In England, there are around 900 businesses per 10,000 population in hamlets, 600 in villages and 400 in urban areas, and in Scotland there are an average 74 start-ups per 10,000 population in rural areas, compared with just 18 in towns and cities.

>When you are the boss

The UK is now a nation of entrepreneurs. All those overnight dotcom success stories, the people who made millions with an idea and a bit of internet knowledge but no experience, left a legacy that has been built on by the surprise popularity of TV shows such as *The Apprentice* and *Dragons' Den*. The message is that you don't need an MBA and a wardrobe full of suits to run your own business. Anyone can have a go. And the easy availability of the communication and office technology to launch a company or run a franchise from home has made that a reality. The self-employed make up 43 % of all teleworkers, as opposed to just 11 % of workers in general.

It is never truer that every penny counts, than when setting up a business. One in five start-ups in the UK fail within the first 12 months. The huge financial commitment that comes with external premises, with mortgage repayments or rent and all the inevitable running costs can easily be the millstone that drags you under. Investing in your own home if you are building, converting or even just decorating a room to be your office, in contrast, can add anything from £2,500 to upwards of £25,000 to its value and provide you with a great, stylish environment that may double up as more than just a workspace.

>The right choice?

So homeworking can make you happier, healthier and wealthier, whether you're employee, employer or head of your own one-person business. Before you trade in the spare bed for a desk and futon, though, you need to look honestly at your own personality and ambitions, your job or company, and your home and the people who share it. While the majority of those who take the leap are evangelical about the benefits, a few people feel lonely and isolated, working longer hours than they ever did in the office, stuck part-way up the career ladder, or close to divorce.

Is homeworking right for you?

Why do you want to be based at home? If you hate your boss, your colleagues and the nature of your work, then a new location is obviously only going to be a temporary fix. It's a new job you need. If you currently leave home in the dark and return in the dark, even in the middle of summer, is it because you're battling with a killer commute or an impossibly heavy workload? Does your solution lie in delegation, outsourcing or a frank conversation with management rather than homeworking *per se*?

Will you actually enjoy it? While some people feel like released prisoners when they leave behind the infamous water-cooler conversations and compulsory team lunches, others are desperately emailing for the latest news by the start of their first afternoon at home. If you number your colleagues among your friends and see the people as one of the perks of your job, or pride yourself on being at least a cabinet member in office politics, then forfeiting that day-to-day social element may well prove to have been a sacrifice too far. In surveys of established homeworkers, isolation is frequently cited as the single biggest downside.

Do you have the discipline to put in the effort without anyone looking over your shoulder — and, just as importantly, to switch off after hours? Natural procrastinators often find themselves falling behind or working later into the night than ever because they have whiled away the day sorting out the laundry, reading the papers and tidying their new office space. At the other end of the spectrum, the element of homeworking most commonly named the hardest to get right is separating work from home life. Whether because of a determination to prove they are still pulling their weight, poor time management, or a tendency towards workaholism, many homeworkers keep their computers running almost literally 24 hours a day, replying instantly to late-night emails and logging on again before they've even boiled the kettle in the morning.

If your primary motivation is the desire to save money, do some very careful calculations of your own circumstances, and be aware of the hidden costs of homeworking. Yes, the increased heating, electricity and telephone bills are offset by sometimes huge savings on petrol and rail season tickets, but typically there are also more expensive insurance premiums to pay, plus IT support, maintenance and repairs, and equipment and software upgrades, not to mention the initial outlay on office furniture and technology. Some people will also face business rates, plus capital gains tax if they sell their property in future. In one survey, 7 % of homeworkers admitted their costs were actually greater than when they worked in a shared office.

Working from home can be fantastic – for you, your family and your business – but don't turn it into a fantasy. J K Rowling may have written the first *Harry Potter* book with her baby daughter sleeping beside her, but unless you are intending to work part-time, don't make the mistake of thinking you can cut back on childcare because you will be there to look after the kids yourself. With school-age children, most parents succeed in wangling it for the odd bank holiday, but when it comes to half terms and longer breaks, nobody tries it more than once.

Is it right for your work?

What stage have you reached in your career? There are exceptions, but working from home can be a definite disadvantage when starting out. Even if a training structure is in place, in the early stages everyone learns informally, by osmosis from more experienced colleagues close by. The social side to office life – the lunches and the impromptu quick drink after work that becomes an all-night session – can be invaluable in creating a team spirit and keeping everyone abreast of company circumstances. If you've already built those relationships, it's perfectly possible to keep them going by phone and email without regularly meeting in person, but if you haven't, you will probably remain an outsider. Not only will you be the last to hear about upcoming positions, departures, promotions and redundancies, but when it comes to the big decisions, there is a danger you will be overlooked or somehow seen as less integral to the company.

Whether that is a risk worth taking obviously depends on your own feelings about the job and aspirations for the future. Even if you're well established in your career and the company policy is officially supportive of homeworking, what is the personal attitude of your immediate superiors and colleagues? If you are self-employed, is it within an industry where operating from home will possibly still raise some eyebrows among potential clients? It is a sad fact that some people continue to associate office-based employment with hard work and professionalism – and homeworking with the opposite. One high-profile MP recently attracted an outcry and also an alarming number of messages of support with his, albeit deliberately provocative, statement that homeworking is '*a euphemism for sloth, apathy, staring out of the window and random surfing of the internet*'. According to surveys, around a sixth of homeworkers believe they will experience less career progression. Fortunately, these are attitudes that will probably die out over the next few years and eventually be seen as laughably outdated as working from home becomes more commonplace.

Some jobs will self-evidently never be done from home. Others that look perfectly adaptable on paper may prove more of a challenge in reality. What is the meeting culture in your company? There is an old joke – typically to be found printed on mugs at the back of the cupboard in office kitchens – '*We're going to keep having these meetings every day until we find out why no work is getting done*'. Sound painfully familiar? Homeworkers who try to escape that kind of environment have in some cases found that they are dragged back into the office for face-to-face discussions on such a regular basis that they end up doing most of their work there. The only difference is that they no longer have their own desk. Formally or informally, do you perform a mentor role to other staff in the office? Technology, from videoconferencing facilities and instant messaging to old-fashioned phone lines, can keep you in more or less constant contact, but in general terms, the more autonomous your job within the company, the easier homeworking will be in practice.

If any of the above are real issues for employees and employers, a flexible working schedule could be the perfect compromise solution. Indeed, among employed teleworkers, doing one or two days a week from home is the most popular arrangement.

Is it right for your home?

Is your home big enough to serve a dual function? Unless you have the luxury of a self-contained annexe – with its own delivery entrance – that you can devote to your business interests, it is hard to overestimate the impact your work set-up will have on the household as a whole. If you don't have a separate area to serve at least part-time as your office (whether it's the guest room, the attic or the garage), and are relying instead on shared space, the viability of any homeworking plans will be heavily dependent on others. Compact technology and clever storage devices make it perfectly plausible to create a desk area that will all but disappear when you've finished for the day, folding into the wall or away into a cupboard, sliding under existing furniture or doubling up as a dining or side table. That's going to be

little help, though, if you're making important business calls and your partner's trying to have a lie-in, your flatmate's cooking for friends or your two-year-old is playing with her mini music-maker kit right by your chair.

Even if the physical space is available, are your timetables and other requirements compatible? If the nature of your work means there's going to be a constant parade of couriers coming to the door, the phone line will be continually engaged and you will be demanding that dinner is delayed and the television is kept on mute, anyone else in the house is clearly going to lose patience rapidly. Similarly, if you are intending to conduct meetings with colleagues or clients in your home office, you will need to make sure the dirty washing pile and your towel-wrapped, fresh-from-the shower teenager are out of the way.

Obviously many of these obstacles are automatically bypassed if you live alone, but cabin fever is a genuine issue for those in that position. A significant number of home-alone homeworkers, particularly those in a studio flat, complain of feeling less like they work from home and more like they sleep in their office.

You will need to check that the location of your house as well as the building itself will support your job or business. Is there a danger that the address will put off potential clients? Is it accessible for face-to-face meetings? Is the broadband speed available sufficient for your needs? While there are numerous practical steps that can be taken to overcome these issues, from a PO box to membership of external business facilities and various private communications upgrades, these aren't always convenient or cheap.

You will also need to check the legal situation regarding your property. There are currently no clear regulations when it comes to informing your mortgage provider that you intend to work from home, unless you are actually extending the building or changing its definition from a residential dwelling to business premises. However, private rental agreements occasionally stipulate that no work can be done, usually in circumstances where the landlord lives in the same block or is a neighbour. Social housing tenants, too, are sometimes subject to contracts that prevent them from working from home without written permission or, in some cases, at all.

There are a few further potential negative implications of homeworking, regularly trotted out by the doomsayers – security issues if work and sensitive data are being transmitted via the internet, for example. These are all perfectly avoidable if working systems are set up properly from the start. In that case, straightforward precautions such as using a virtual private network and externally stored back-up would make a teleworker no more vulnerable than anyone working in a large office.

Homeworking isn't for everyone, and it calls for a lot of planning and organisation, both in advance and on a day-to-day basis. Knowing what to buy, how to make the most of the space you have, and tried-and-tested ways to avoid domestic discord and the time-management traps – plus vital facts about your home office and the law – can help you create a set-up that will serve you well for as long as you choose to telework. And having made the move, not many people go back.

Finally, as a homeworker, you will also have to accept two things. First, there will be people – contrary to all the evidence – who will never believe you do anything other than get up late, watch daytime television and answer the odd email in your pyjamas. Second, there will come a time, almost certainly perilously close to a deadline, when your computer refuses to cooperate any more and you are forced to admit that far from being the incompetent, socially inept dungeon-dweller you always maintained he was, the IT guy actually ranks somewhere between genius and God. If you can do that, then congratulations! More than half of homeworkers say they are in their dream job, so read on to help make your experience as smooth and successful as possible.

Setting the budget

2

Can you afford to work from home? The answer is a resounding yes. Whether you are in a position to take the financial gamble on setting up your own business or quitting your job to go freelance is a different question, but everyone can successfully budget for homeworking. You can dispel any student memories of shivering at your desk in three jumpers in an attempt to stave off the heating bill too. With a little bit of planning, you can work from a home office that is warm, well lit, attractively decorated, ergonomically furnished and kitted out with all the technology you need – without breaking the bank. You should also be able to pay for utilities, communications and business travel, and still have money left over to celebrate your homeworking success. After all, if only 7 % of homeworkers have claimed that their costs are actually higher than they were when they commuted to the office, that means 93 % are paying out either roughly the same amount or less – in some cases considerably less.

The single most important measure is to make all the relevant calculations in advance. Your options will be limited once you are faced with a bill you don't have the wherewithal to pay, whereas it is relatively easy to keep costs within a budget when you are setting up and fitting out your new home office. Depending on your financial situation, the cash flow required for your business and any specific upcoming expenditure you are aware of, it might just be a matter of postponing non-essential software upgrades or the re-decoration of the office walls. Seeing the figures in black and white may also stop you embarking on an ambitious renovation or construction project to create your home workspace, at least in the short term. This could potentially free up tens of thousands of pounds for use elsewhere.

>The savings

First, the uplifting bit. Do the sums and work out what you are going to save by working from home. Don't overlook purchases such as office shirts or dismiss the little everyday costs. You may be astounded at how much you spend on take-away Americanos in a year.

Travel

According to Work Wise UK (www.workwiseuk.org), a not-for-profit initiative that champions flexible working practices and is the driving force behind the annual Work Wise Week and National Work from Home Day, the typical UK road commuter does a 27km (17 mile) round trip to the office, costing an average £7 in fuel. With the rising price of petrol and some people driving considerably greater distances to work, your bill could be double or even treble that. Add in the cost of parking, and the congestion charge if your office is in central London, and you could be paying upwards of £500 a month on road travel alone. On average, commuting accounts for a quarter of the total cost of owning and running a car in the UK.

The price of train travel at peak times has also escalated in the past few years. Fares are expected to rise by around 5% a year until 2014, which can mean an increase on some commuter lines of over £350 for an annual season ticket. Also factor in the cost of the taxi when you leave the office late. For employees who commute any distance, travel is almost certainly their single biggest expenditure over the year. So it's a saving that will have a major impact.

Meals

Many people take a packed lunch every morning, but it's not unusual for commuters to buy a coffee and a bacon sandwich at the station, lunch in the canteen, local pub or sandwich shop, and then a mid-afternoon caffeine boost

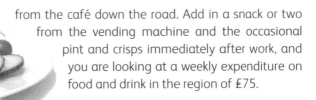

from the café down the road. Add in a snack or two from the vending machine and the occasional pint and crisps immediately after work, and you are looking at a weekly expenditure on food and drink in the region of £75.

Business clothes

If your office policy is the usual smart casual, the switch to homeworking isn't going to make a dent in your clothes shopping budget. But for those working in industries where suits are still *de rigueur*, not having to pay for expensive tailoring – plus appropriate shoes, shirts and other accessories – for daily use could save well over £1,000 a year

External premises

For most people who are self-employed or launching or running their own business, the only viable alternative to homeworking is buying or renting separate office space. While this obviously has several advantages – from additional room and greater potential for expansion and taking on staff, to a professional working environment and the social element – it is also a massive drain on finances. By opting to be home-based instead, you will be saving money in numerous ways.

▶ Monthly rent or mortgage repayments: Even in the current uncertain property market, a domestic mortgage normally has lower interest rates and better terms than a commercial one.
▶ Separate utilities bills: Your household costs will obviously go up if you are working there, but the overall outgoings will still be smaller than those needed for heating, lighting and powering a second premises.
▶ Additional IT equipment, broadband connection and phone lines: Assuming you would want at least an internet-enabled laptop at home.

▶ Business rates on your work premises: In most circumstances, you wouldn't need to pay these on a home office, which would instead be covered by your normal council tax bill.

▶ A second insurance policy: It is cheaper to extend your household policy to cover your business interests than to take out separate cover.

▶ Travelling between your home and work premises.

Save money working at home:

- ◯ Little or no travel costs
- ◯ No more take away coffees or unplanned lunches out
- ◯ Less expenditure on business clothing
- ◯ Lower outgoings than renting premises for a business
- ◯ Potentially reduced home expenses

Home expenses

This is a grey area because you should only offset expenses and save paying the tax on items and utilities that you need for business use. However, in practice many people find that their personal expenditure is reduced because there is inevitable overlap. Discuss the details of your individual situation with your accountant before making any large office purchases or submitting your tax return if you are self-employed, or visit the HM Revenue & Customs website (www.hmrc.gov.uk) for more information.

>The costs

Your outgoings as a homeworker can be divided into the initial one-off or infrequent costs related to setting up your home office as a pleasant working environment with all the equipment you need, and the ongoing payments on utility bills, communication, insurance, tax and any support services such as IT or external back-up that you might outsource.

If you are an employee, your first move should obviously be to establish precisely what your employer will provide or reimburse you for. If homeworking is an established concept at your company and actively encouraged or even required, there will probably be a system in place. Typically employers provide computers already loaded with software necessary to your job. However, if you are being offered a laptop and are going to be working from home more than one day a week, you should negotiate at the very least a contribution towards a desktop PC. It is generally not good for your eyes or posture to be working long hours at a laptop, and your employer has a legal responsibility to meet your Health & Safety requirements even when you are working remotely (see Chapter 7 for guidelines on safe computer use and Chapter 11 for more information on employers' obligations towards homeworkers). Some companies will also provide a desk and office chair, or money towards their purchase. Again, check that any equipment you are given is suitable for your job. Some manufacturers and retailers classify desk chairs according to the number of hours of use per day that they have been designed for.

What an employer generally won't contribute towards is the cost of creating and decorating your home workspace and fitting it with appropriate lighting, shelving and so on. Your company should, however, cover all your business-related calls and other reasonable expenses. You need to agree a system for this: reimbursement of strictly itemised bills or a mutually acceptable monthly amount, or installing a completely separate business line in your home office.

If you requested the chance to homework from a less than enthusiastic employer, you might have to fight harder to recover the expenses you are entitled to. In one survey, 93% of people said it was individual employees rather than the company pushing for homeworking, and only 40% stated that their employer covered the costs of remote working. Do agree terms in advance and get them down in writing, and keep bills, receipts and other evidence of all your work-related outgoings

If you are self-employed or running your own business, your only restriction is what you can or are willing to pay – though you should be aware of exactly what expenditure you can offset against your tax. With everything, from the location and design of your home office to furniture, technology and communications packages, the range of options – and prices – is vast. How you choose what is best for you in all these areas is covered in detail elsewhere in this book. If you are just starting out, you may not yet be in a position to make a decision on all the areas, but always allow for the maximum you might spend when working out the budget. However, remember that there are often less expensive temporary measures you can take to allow you to spread the cost

Setting up

Be realistic about not only what will suit you, your household and the nature of your work, but what you can comfortably afford. If you have set your heart on a loft conversion or an eco-friendly garden office, consider whether there is also space that could work in the interim. That way you can give homeworking a trial run before ploughing large amounts of money into it, concentrate your efforts and finances on getting your business up and running (if that's what you are doing), and break down that initial outlay into more manageable instalments. See Chapter 3 for tips on identifying suitable space within your existing home, at least in the short term.

There are some purchases you will have to make, such as a computer with relevant software. If you are going to be spending several hours a day in front of it, it is important to invest in an appropriate, ergonomically designed chair from the start. Otherwise you will risk having ongoing back and other musculoskeletal problems. Proper lighting is also essential to avoid eyestrain and headaches, but it is possible to create this with relatively cheap freestanding lamps and spotlights and save mounting more expensive permanent uplighters and downlighters until you have the cash available.

You won't have to pay tax on a computer given to you by your employer, but if the company reimburses you for the cost of your office equipment, the situation depends on how it registers these expenses. If they are reported as benefits in kind, tax may need to be paid. If you buy a computer from your employer, you can claim 25 % of its net value for four years as business expenses. Self-employed homeworkers are entitled to capital allowances on designated business equipment and fixtures.

The Inland Revenue has to be convinced that anything employees try to claim is a genuine business expense and deemed necessary by their employer. If you have requested to work from home rather than being expected or required to by your company, this is harder to prove. If you already have a phone line and broadband connection for your personal use, it's highly unlikely that you can claim the installation costs and you should only put in for a reasonable proportion of the ongoing bills. Other utilities bills may be a stumbling block if you are still employed. Those who are self-employed or operating a home-based business can again offset a reasonable portion of these running costs, but the necessity of heating and lighting for solely business use is hard to justify if you have the option of being in the office. Go through your circumstances with your accountant or employer or look at www.hmrc.gov.uk so you are clear on where you stand.

Utilities bills

Studies show that there is a typical rise of around 14 % on energy bills once an occupant starts working from home. This obviously will depend on the quantity and consumption levels of technology in your office and the measures you take to reduce usage. Be particularly aware of spiralling heating costs if your home office is separate from the main living areas of the house in a garage or loft conversion, for example, or if the property is particularly large, poorly insulated or has an old, inefficient heating system. Environmental campaigners have recently argued that although homeworking is the greener option during the summer months, the average rise in energy consumption over the winter cancels out all the advantages, so fitting individual thermostats so that you are heating only the room you are using could make a big difference. If you are self-employed and plan to claim part of your heating costs against tax, you should either have a metered supply or base your calculations on the square metres of room space used for business compared with those heated overall during your working hours.

Tax

The vast majority of homeworkers continue to pay council tax as they did before. However, if you have turned any part of your property into wholly business or commercial premises, you could be liable for business rates on that room or area alone. This holds true whether it is a guest bedroom or a garage, but won't apply if you still have a bed for visitors alongside your desk or a lawnmower stored in the

corner. The criteria are very specific and in practice only really come into play if you are flagging up the changed nature of the building with a commercial sign, separate access, a significantly increased volume of traffic to the door or similar.

See Chapter 11 for more details. If you do have to pay business rates, that portion of your home will be taken out of your council tax assessment, which may or may not bring it down a band. Visit the Valuation Office Agency website (www.voa.gov.uk and www.mybusinessrates.gov.uk) for an idea of the probable cost on your set-up. Remember that if part of your home is rated as business premises, you may have to pay capital gains tax on that percentage of the property if you come to sell it.

With the parameters for what constitutes business and domestic areas within a home somewhat flexible to say the least, potential homeworkers are frequently advised simply to stay quiet about the fact. If there are no external or visible consequences of your decision to work from home, that isn't necessarily hard to do. But there are advantages to declaring part of your home an office. If you are self-employed, you can offset not only the business-related portions of your utilities bills and equipment costs (including consumables such as toner cartridges and paper), but also rent or mortgage interest and council tax, all apportioned by the number of rooms or square metres allocated to business and the percentage of time used. That does change, though, if you got a mortgage top-up, specifically to create a home office so consult your accountant in that instance.

Definition:

Capital gains tax:

Capital gains tax (CGT) is payable on the profit you make when selling eligible assets, over and above your annual CGT allowance which for 2008/09 is £9,600. Your main home is usually exempt but if you have been using part of it as business premises – normally indicated by paying business rates rather than council tax – then CGT will be payable on that portion of the property. The government has recently, and controversially, changed the amounts involved and a range of reliefs are available. Find out more at www.hmrc.gov.uk/cgt.

Support services

As an employee, support services required should be minimal as you will still have access to the full team in the main office for IT back-up, human resources, publicity and marketing, and other expertise. Your company may even contribute towards cleaning your home office, though most employees find that they do have to swallow some costs generated by working remotely. If you have gone freelance or have your own business, you are responsible for all these areas. Some you will obviously take on yourself – though if they are time-consuming there may still be a financial price in terms of hours away from your main role – and others you might pay someone else to do. Small businesses usually have a marketing and advertising budget because it is hard to reach customers without at least some expenditure. So it isn't uncommon for even one-person start-ups to have an account with an external public relations company. An increasing number of self-employed workers set up in their own homes are outsourcing aspects of their IT, digital filing and communications. Backing up on to CDs, DVDs or a second hard drive can be laborious and you still need a secure place to keep them in case of fire, flooding or theft. It may be safer and more convenient and cheaper to use the automatic back-up via online providers (also known as digital vaults).

Unless you are technically minded or work in IT, you will also need recourse to outside help during the technology crisis that every homeworker dreads. Emergency call-outs tend to be expensive and often turn out to have been unnecessary. For the purposes of budgeting, you will have to predict how often you might require such a service, based on the age and quality of your machine, the demands you are making of it and your own technical know-how. You can then build in a financial buffer for this purpose, or sign up to an IT support contract, which for a fixed fee will typically cover unlimited telephone support, help via remote access and on-site assistance if all else fails. Some also cover routine checks and maintenance as a preventive measure.

The costs of working at home:

- Potentially increased utility bills
- The cost of creating a suitable work space
- The cost of installing all necessary equipment
- Support services – IT support, accountant, couriers
- Extra time to perform all tasks without office support – post, filing, photocopying
- Insurance for work space and equipment

Any fees you pay to an accountant or solicitor need to be factored in here, too.

Insurance

Check that the equipment supplied to you by your employer is covered by a company insurance policy. If you are self-employed, you will at the very least need to add any new office equipment to your household policy. Usually though, you will have to either pay for a homeworking extension to your existing cover or take out a separate specialist policy. Include any additional costs for supplementary cover – for example, the basic policy will not always cover laptops when away from home.

>What do the figures mean for you?

Once you have deducted your running costs as a homeworker (excluding one-off set-up payments) from your regular expenditure previously, you should have a much clearer idea of the effect working from home will have on your bank balance. This obviously takes no account of your income – either salary and sales or other financial sources including grants and personal or business loans – or any additional outgoings associated with your specific business, such as payments to suppliers or manufacturing and distribution costs. It is simply a comparison of the main costs of working in an office and at home, and will show what savings you can expect to make on a daily, weekly, quarterly and more long-term basis. You can therefore see before you spend a penny whether you are in a position to pay upfront for your dream home office, whether it is a financially sound decision to take out a loan and pay it back over a set time frame, or whether you need to work with what you have for the moment.

If your calculations indicate that being home-based will actually cost you more than going to the office every morning – which is possible, particularly if your commute is free and you are already very money conscious when it comes to all those forgotten extras – then you can look at instigating cost-cutting measures from the start. See Chapter 12 for ideas of how to save money on everything from essential furniture and equipment to communications and utilities bills.

>Money management

If you intend to run your own business, particularly if you are seeking any form of outside funding, you need a full business plan, including details of your predicted cashflow patterns for at least the first year, your expected income, and profit and loss forecasts for three to five years. It can be useful to run through the basic elements – the facts and figures rather than the inherently optimistic projections – for your personal information and planning. There are heavy tomes on how to put together a business plan but if you just want a checklist of the fundamentals, visit www.businesslink.gov.uk or look at more than 100 free samples covering virtually every type of business at www.bplans. co.uk.

You can create your own financial planner over every relevant time period: daily and weekly running costs; monthly and quarterly bills and loan repayments; annual insurance premiums and tax expenditure if you are self-employed; and more occasional but predictable outgoings such as software upgrades. You can download a free automated budget planner from www.money-savingexpert.com. It might sound like a hassle, but you will make the most of

Definition:

Business plan:
A business plan is put together before a new start-up is launched, both to help secure outside investment from a bank or other source, and to give all those involved with the company a clear idea of where it is heading. It should cover the business objectives and strategies, the market it will operate in, and detailed – and informed – financial forecasts.

your money by setting up separate accounts for each of these as appropriate. If you file a tax return, for example, you will know that you will require a lump sum to pay to the Inland Revenue by the end of January each year. It is vital that you put enough money aside to cover this. As you won't need access to this money at any other time look for a relatively high-interest savings account with limited withdrawals, for example, a card-less account where you have to give notice to take money out over the counter will offer far more generous terms than one without restrictions. If you are confident of the exact nature of any tax breaks or credits and the expenses you will be able to offset then you can deduct it accordingly before you pay money into your designated tax savings. If not, then strictly setting aside the full percentage from every paid invoice will leave you with a useful buffer that will also earn decent interest.

You will obviously need a current account for all the everyday expenses, and some experts recommend setting up a separate one as a dedicated bills fund. You can then arrange for at least some of your utilities payments to be made by direct debit, which sometimes carries a discount. It is vital to have an emergency fund, which should again be in an account that you can access 24/7. The amount you will need varies depending on your circumstances. Financial advisers suggest looking at the costs of a temporary solution to a range of possible problems from theft of your laptop to your printer breaking down or your home requiring emergency repairs. Then try to ensure that your fund contains enough money to cover the highest of these potential costs with a little bit extra for the inevitable financial side effects of a situation like that.

It worked for me...

Fran, 32, Winchester

Fran has been working from home for a year. She says:

'I didn't consider any financial benefits of working from home before I started – I just wanted to get away from crowded trains that always seemed to be delayed, and sitting in a depressing, grey, air-conditioned box all day every day. But I started to notice the difference very quickly.

I used to have to stop at the cash machine almost every day to get money for lunch or a quick drink after work or something to eat on the train home. Now I do one big supermarket shop at the weekend, and that's it. That weekly shop is, admittedly, quite a lot more expensive than it used to be, partly because I'm stocking up on food for breakfast and lunch that I rarely had at home and partly because I do treat myself to snacks for when I need perking up mid-afternoon. They're only about a third of the price of the things I used to get from the office canteen, though, and they're definitely healthier.

I did have to extend my overdraft to buy everything I wanted to get up and running, including an MFD and a new desk chair and shelves. At the times each month when I would have been renewing my season ticket for the train, I was instantly £400 better off, so I wish I'd spaced out those purchases instead and just made do in the meantime. I had an old printer that still worked and I could have carried on using the windowsill for my books and files for a little bit longer!

My phone bill the first month was extortionate, but after that I got organised, switched tariffs to one with a flat fee for all UK landline calls and started arranging for my overseas clients to call me at set times. I looked at switching my electricity provider but I couldn't find anything that was going to be more than £10 cheaper over a year, so I'm just making an effort to switch everything off when I'm not using it and have the radiators on only in my office and kitchen during the day.'

The other essential is a savings buffer. Many people combine this with their emergency fund, but it can earn greater interest in a separate savings account. Also, it helps to ensure there is always some money held in reserve in case ill fortune strikes again before you have

'I had an old printer that still worked and I could have carried on using the windowsill for my books and files for a little bit longer!'

had a chance to rebuild your fund. You don't need instant access to your savings buffer because it isn't for use in an immediate crisis but to help you through difficult periods, such as if you are self-employed and off sick or you lose your job. Most experts advise having a buffer of between three and six months of living expenses, though you will have to keep saving if you want it to cover your ongoing business costs at the same time.

Resources:

Useful websites
Business Link: www.businesslink.gov.uk
HM Revenue & Customs: www.hmrc.gov.uk
The Motley Fool: www.fool.co.uk
Startups: www.startups.co.uk

Further reading
▶ *The Everything Budgeting Book* by Tere Stouffer (Adams Media Corporation)

This American book is packed with practical advice for controlling personal, family and household finances.

▶ *The Financial Times Guide to Business Start Up 2008* by Sara Williams (Financial Times/Prentice Hall)

The annually updated guide, considered a bible by many small-business owners, covers finance, tax and law in easy-to-understand detail.

▶ *Start Your Business: Week by Week* by Steve Parks (Prentice Hall)

A step-by-step walk through the first six months of launching a business, complete with checklists and useful contact information for all aspects including financial planning.

How to get started

A look in any estate agent window will show that properties are increasingly being sold with a home office as part of the package. All too often that's just jargon, a phrase used, rather like nursery has been for decades, to describe a space too small to be reasonably called a bedroom. However, things have changed since the study was inevitably the tiniest room in the house; the last corner left when every other bit of space had been claimed. With home offices no longer used just in the evenings and on occasional weekends but, for a growing number of people, the single room in which they will spend the greatest amount of time, their status in the house is rising. Those who have made a commitment to homeworking often take it as an opportunity to reassess how the space in their property is used – or even to do the renovation or building work they may have been considering. With the UK housing market currently in a state of uncertainty, experts are seeing more and more people choose to make changes to their existing homes to accommodate their needs rather than looking to move.

Clearly if you live in a flat or rent your home, your options are more limited, but even if you have to work with what you already have, the most obvious place for your office may not necessarily be the best. It can be very helpful to dig out the floor plans of the property from the time at which you moved in and look at them as a blank canvas. If you have made the decision to regularly work from home you will probably already have earmarked your potential office, but aside from immovables such as the kitchen, bathroom and plumbed-in utility areas, try to avoid instantly labelling any room. Look not just at the current internal rooms but the comparative dimensions and location of any garage or outbuildings, and at the size, shape and topography of the garden itself. Consider space now being used for storage and you might find you have enough room for a computer desk and some filing.

When you add up the hours you will be spending in your home office – and take into account that you will expect to think clearly, work productively and perhaps be inspired creatively while you are there – it is essential that your needs are met in terms of space, light, technology, noise levels and accessibility and that you like the room. Equally vital, though, if your homeworking is to be successful for you and your family or other householders, is that you don't sacrifice your home in pursuit of the perfect office.

While nobody can work effectively in a cupboard (though plenty of people have tried, and over a third of homeworkers in one recent poll said they operated from a space with no natural light), don't let your job to take over the best and biggest room in the house. If you can't eat, sleep or relax without being confronted by work issues, you will never be able to switch off and your home will no longer be a sanctuary.

According to one survey, more than half of homeworkers are unhappy with their home office – but you don't have to be one of them. Run through the questions and suggestions in this chapter to help identify the most suitable workspace available to you. If you are still uncertain consider calling in the experts. A professional designer will ask about you and your working practices and evaluate any potential office space in the light of your answers, providing the distance and clarity it can be hard to find yourself.

>Inside or outside

The first question is whether to use a room or area inside your house as an office, or create one that is separate from your main home, whether by converting the garage or another outbuilding or putting up a new structure in the garden. The right answer will depend on the nature of your business and your household.

If you expect to hold meetings with clients, colleagues, suppliers and contractors in your office on a regular basis, an external room can be laid out, decorated and furnished with the image you wish to project in mind, and without having to make compromises for anyone else. Meetings will on the whole carry a greater sense of confidentiality and professionalism than they would if held within what is obviously a home.

Even if visitors will be rare or non-existent, a space purely devoted to your work should prove more conducive to productivity and creativity than one playing two or even multiple roles. A garden view, if you have one, and the proximity of greenery and wildlife are believed to contribute to your health and wellbeing, partly because your body can respond naturally to the passing of the seasons – and the hours. An external office also helps to draw a mental line between work and leisure time because you can literally lock it up and go home at the end of the day. Kirsty Allsop, Andrew Marr and, perhaps unsurprisingly, Diarmuid Gavin are among those who enjoy the benefits of working from a garden office. Garden offices are becoming very popular and specialist garden office design and construction companies are reporting increases in sales of between 100% and 700% a year.

The principal downside of an external office of this nature, unless you already have one, is obviously the cost. Setting up in a spare bedroom may cost no more than the price of your furniture and technology, whereas a conversion or purpose-built structure will not only call for an initial outlay that could run into tens of thousands of pounds – or more – but is also likely to cause a greater increase in your household bills. In addition, there is the issue of the time involved – factoring in any planning applications, groundwork, connection of communications lines and decorating as well as the actual construction or renovation – and the possible cost and inconvenience of finding alternative premises to work in during that period.

Of course many people don't have outside space, and it can also seem somewhat contrary to abandon a beautifully furnished and heated home, with all bathroom and kitchen facilities to hand, for the greater part of your day. Also, it isn't always practical as a homeworker to cut yourself off from the workings of the house as a whole. If you have to answer the domestic landline and the front door, feed the dog and check the children have made it back from school, you will probably want to be based in the main home.

Your own personality, the amount of background buzz you can cope with, your attitude towards homeworking and your ability to unwind at other times will be as important as your budget, your job and your family's preferences in making a decision as to what will work for you. To weigh up all the factors, consider the pros and cons of the most common options as outlined below.

Pros and cons...

LIVING ROOM

Pros: Typically the largest room in the house, so perhaps the least likely to be cluttered by the addition of a desk and some filing or other storage units. If it is laid out in such a way that it can be mentally divided into different areas – L-shaped, with large alcoves, or long enough that you can have an office 'end', for example – so much the better. Visually, your workspace will jar less in a room that already has technology in the form of a television screen or music system, as well as bookshelves, in place. You may also be able to use a section of existing shelving for work files.

Like any downstairs space if your home has more than one floor, the living room offers easy access to the front door if you expect regular deliveries as part of your job, but in a shared house it tends to be relatively quiet during the day. As the room designed for relaxing and entertaining, it probably also makes the most of any views and natural light, is well heated and draught-free, and is generally a very pleasant environment in which to spend the greater part of your day.

Cons: It can be difficult to effectively separate work from home life when you sit back with a glass of wine in the evening with your computer and flashing work answerphone in full view. Your job is also impinging on other household members if they want to watch television or use the space during your working hours, particularly if it is the only comfortable living area in the house. By basing yourself in the hub of the home, you will possibly be disturbed by activity in the kitchen and hallways and also by the doorbell if there are lots of non work-related visitors to the property. If it is a large room it will also be expensive to heat all day during the winter.

KITCHEN

Pros: Kitchens tend to be warm, cosy rooms that are easily heated. In a small flat, it might be the most neutral space if you don't want

your work encroaching on your personal life in your bedroom or the living room. Particularly if you live alone, a simple desk can double up as a breakfast table or vice versa.

Cons: Neither IT equipment nor paperwork stands up well to steamy conditions or the greasy residues that are inevitable if you are cooking and eating within the same small space. Kitchens are also the most dangerous places in the house to have trailing wires, so even if you want to work in there, you will probably have to find an alternative home for your printer and filing, and use a laptop with fully wireless technology. Unless you have a huge kitchen with a back door, they can easily get stuffy and often have little natural light. You are also likely to be continually distracted by dirty dishes, other householders wanting to make coffee or lunch, and the noise of the washing machine.

BEDROOM

Pros: Very quiet during the day and physically removed from the hustle and bustle of the main living areas. The main bedroom would almost certainly be the largest of the upstairs rooms, and may also be well equipped with fitted cupboards and other storage options so your paperwork at least can be easily hidden away. The décor, lighting and ambience are likely to make it a calm space to think in. It's also nice to keep any social visitors totally removed from your work environment – and not to have to worry about your children's friends spilling something on your keyboard or important documents.

Cons: Any sleep expert will tell you that the bedroom should be a refuge, with no television and certainly no fully fledged office at the foot of the bed. It can be difficult to switch off mentally if you can see next day's work pile from your pillow, and anyone sending you a fax late at night will be picturing it whirring in an empty office, not waking you up. If you have a partner, are there going to be clashes if they want a lie-in on a day off or are feeling ill and need to be in bed? What if you have to work into the early hours to meet a deadline? Also, while soft lighting can be peaceful and romantic in the bedroom, it's not suitable for long hours in front of the computer and may lead to eye strain.

GUEST BEDROOM

Pros: Tucked away from the daily to-ings and fro-ings of the house and not invading communal living space. If there is no designated room available to act as an office then, unless you have a never-ending stream of guests, this may well be the next best thing.

Cons: It may be quite a squeeze to fit in a desk and office equipment as well as a bed, though a futon or sofa bed can help. But what will you do when you or other members of the household have people to stay? Where will you store your paperwork, especially if confidentiality is a big issue? Do you have a laptop so you can retreat to a back-up workspace while guests are in residence? The bedroom will inevitably have something of the feel of an office and won't be such a welcoming space for visitors. As little space goes to waste in most hectic family homes, there is a good chance the guest bedroom is already serving a dual function, whether it's full of drying clothes or being used for storage.

HALL OR LANDING

Pros: In a small or busy home, this is often the only unused space. Depending on the layout, it needn't restrict access and you are not taking an entire room out of use for others during working hours.

Cons: It can be distracting if you are set up in a busy thoroughfare, as well as inconvenient to others in the house who don't want to interrupt you. Your work materials will probably be on full view 24/7. There may be a shortage of power points. Open spaces such as this can have echoes, which, combined with the lack of doors, can make it difficult to make private business calls or block the noise of activity in other rooms.

CONSERVATORY

Pros: A conservatory can be a lovely working environment in the right weather, with loads of natural light, which is good for your eyes and wellbeing and boosts feel-good hormones. Conservatories usually offer a good view both out into the garden and back inside the house through glass doors, making it easier to keep an eye on children or pets when necessary.

Cons: Many conservatories are difficult to heat economically in winter and keep cool in summer, and rain on the roof can be noisy, drowning out phone calls. There are security implications to having all your IT equipment and important documents in a room where they are 'on show' and probably more vulnerable to a break-in. It could also be considered a waste of a conservatory to use it as an office, when it could perhaps be better used for relaxing, dining or as a playroom – certainly other family members may think so.

AN INTERNAL 'ROOM'

You can divide an existing room to create a dedicated office area, for example by creating a mezzanine level if there is sufficient headroom or putting up a partition wall.

Pros: An additional 'room' can give designated office space in return for relatively minor construction work compared with an extension or new building. It probably won't need any kind of planning application. You can be as closed off or integrated into the main body of the house as you wish by choosing a glass partition, large internal window, open balustrade on the mezzanine area, or something far more solid. If the structure and materials allow, it can be designed from the start with maximum soundproofing, ideally located power sockets and lighting sources, etc.

Cons: The costs involved can still be considerable. Few rooms really have the space available to make this work successfully. Even if it suits your needs, breaking a living room down into two very small areas is likely to lessen its appeal and detract from its value if you want to sell in the future.

Pros and cons...

LOFT CONVERSION

Pros: If your house is suitable, a loft conversion is generally viewed as the most economic and efficient method of gaining substantial extra space. Unless your circumstances or intentions are particularly unusual, you shouldn't have to seek planning permission and, depending on the current flooring, insulation, ventilation and skylights, it may not be as expensive as you expect. In most cases it will also add significantly to the value of your property. You will be separate from the rest of the house and remain undisturbed until you choose to come down.

Cons: If your work relies on a lot of deliveries, it is impractical to be running downstairs from the very top of the house every time someone rings the doorbell – and that's if you hear it at all. Attic rooms are often the hottest/coldest rooms in the house, and heating another whole level will have a notable impact on your bill.

GARAGE CONVERSION

Pros: You can make a psychological distinction between work and home life by physically leaving the house in the morning, and you won't see any of the trappings of your job while you are unwinding outside working hours. Most garages will offer you space for a desk, generous storage and a meeting table and chairs or similar. You will be able to invite clients or colleagues into your office without invading personal or family territory. Conversion of an existing building will be considerably cheaper than erecting something from scratch.

Cons: Unless you really go to town on the conversion, in which case the costs will mount up fast, you will have no water supply and hence no kitchen or toilet facilities. A cheap, basic conversion may also leave you with a building that is difficult to heat and lacks much natural light. If you turn the garage entirely over to work use, you will need to seek planning permission and pay business rates. Your equipment may be less secure than it would be locked in the main body of the house and in some cases the location may affect your insurance cover. Deliveries and visitors will go to the front door, and putting up signs directing them to the garage can influence your planning application.

GARDEN OFFICE

Pros: A garden office can be your own separate workspace, distinct from the house but within close enough reach to use all the facilities and even still be covered by a cordless landline phone. People with a love of the outdoors sing the praises of having a garden office, with a view of greenery and the sound of birds, for boosting their creativity and productivity. By designing and building an office from scratch, you have the opportunity to stamp your personality, and the image of your company, all over it, which can be a huge plus-point if clients visit you at home. It also means you can construct it according to ecological principles or with other specific aims in mind.

Garden offices rarely require planning permission and some structures can actually be moved, so you have the option of taking it with you if you sell up (which could be particularly advantageous if potential buyers would prefer to have more garden space). A shed can also take on a legacy in a way that an office in the spare room – however much time, money, effort and love you have ploughed into it – simply can't. When the author Philip Pullman outgrew his garden office, he gave it to a friend and illustrator on condition that he in turn would pass it to another writer.

Cons: If your garden isn't large, it may be completely dominated by an office, to the detriment of children, pets and your own leisure time, particularly in the summer. Depending on your spec, a garden office can cost anything from under £5,000 for a very basic structure to upwards of £60,000. Although it will usually add value to your house, most experts agree you are unlikely to make back what you spend on it. You may also have to pay extra to get phone and internet access away from the main house. Some insurance companies won't cover timber buildings because of the fire risk. If your garden office will be overlooked or offers a view of neighbours' gardens, it could lead to frayed relations at the least. Many of the benefits of being closer to nature may seem considerably less appealing in the depths of winter when it's cold, wet and windy.

Inside or outside:

○ Limitations of your house – is there space to create a separate area?

○ Is it possible to build a new space within or outside the home?

○ How suitable is the area for meetings and visitors?

○ How practical is it to be based away from the house?

○ How easy will it be to 'shutoff' from the rest of the house if you are based within the home?

○ Can you afford the cost of a new construction?

Time for an extension?

Putting a new extension on your house is unlikely to prove cost-effective if it is simply the addition of an office. Most professional designers recommend looking first at converting any loft space, which typically involves significantly less financial outlay and red tape. If, however, you have been considering an extension in order to get extra living space then the requirement of a home office can help to justify the expense. Again, it is worth looking closely at plans of the property to decide on a new layout – in most cases, the best solution for benefiting the family and adding value to your home is to transform an existing room into your office and create an impressive kitchen, dining or living space in the extension to maximise its potential.

>Getting the builders in

If you have the chance to build an office from scratch or have a loft, garage or outbuilding converted and choose to go down this route, it is a huge commitment to your long-term homeworking plans and one of the biggest investments you are likely to make. The growing popularity of homeworking means there are now more companies specialising in offices in your home and garden, which should make the task easier. You should get at least three quotes for the work (the 'Find a domestic builder' search facility on the National Federation of Builders website at www.builders.org.uk is useful). Before signing up with any contractor you should ask the following questions:

▶ Can you see previous examples of their work?

▶ Can they supply references from satisfied clients?

▶ How does their design and planning process work? Can you be involved as you would like?

▶ What is their specific area of expertise?

▶ How do they wish to be paid; in stages or on completion?

▶ Will they agree to a retention clause, where part of the payment is held back until any faults in the finished work are put right?

▶ Will they give a final completion date and accept a penalty clause should they fail to meet this? This could be essential if you are forking out for other work premises in the meantime or are forced to miss out on business because you have no office.

► Do they bring links to a team of other professionals you may need such as carpenters, electricians and decorators? If so, what are their credentials? Most services have their own accreditation bodies, and you should always look out for the Trust Mark, which signifies government-endorsed standards.

You also need to check independently whether a planning application will be required and you should be aware of how Building Regulations apply to what you are having done. See Chapter 11 for more details on the legal aspects of planning and construction. Try to stay open-minded about the exact dimensions and site of a garden office or other new structure until you have consulted fully with the professionals. Shaving a few inches off the roof or moving it a little further from a boundary fence or closer to the house might make all the difference in getting a planning application approved or not needing one in the first place. There are also factors such as soil type, gradients and the course of any underground pipes and cables that might make the location you have earmarked unsuitable or extremely challenging.

You will obviously pay a lot more for a complete package including all the fixtures, fittings and final touches, and for a site supervisor, but it is worth doing the calculations in detail before you decide whether or not it would be money well spent. If you intend to oversee operations yourself, you will obviously have to be present at least some of the time. Don't underestimate how often problems and queries will take you away from your work – and that is if you are able to concentrate or make phone calls at all with a construction site outside the window. You also need some degree of knowledge of the building process. It will drag on for weeks if you don't coordinate everyone involved to ensure that cables are put in before flooring goes down and so on. It may well be better overall to swallow the cost, put someone else in charge of the construction work, and either postpone the start date for your homeworking or rent some office space short term if it is available locally.

>Planning and design

There is a huge amount that can be done in decorating and furnishing a room to create the perfect working environment can require a lot of work. However, if you can design it as you wish from an earlier stage, bear the following in mind:

► How can you optimise natural light? Could you use a combination of skylights and windows to keep the room bright for as much of the day as possible?

There's no point in having an office bathed in sunlight in the early morning if you don't start work until later, when the sun has moved round and it's so dark you need to switch lights on.

▶ Are there going to be enough power points and telephone sockets, and will they be where you need them? It may be conventional to put sockets on opposite walls, but there is nothing to stop you adding extra in one area if you know that's where all your technology will be located. Do consider possible extras such as lamps, electric heaters and even a small fridge as well as your office equipment.

▶ How easy is it going to be to keep your office warm in winter and cool in summer. Discuss the quality of insulation, siting of radiators and type of ventilation with the designers before any work is underway.

▶ Are you intending to have built-in storage? If the room is square or rectangular, movable storage units are far more flexible, but where there are alcoves and sloping roof sections, creating permanent shelving and cupboards is usually the best way to use the space.

▶ Do you have any options when it comes to access? If the room is on the ground floor, what would be the implications of putting in your own entrance, separate to the main door of the house? If there is a clear route out to the road or parking area, this could be a godsend if you expect a lot of work-related visitors. Homeworkers who have some outdoor space where they can work when the weather permits, even if it's just a plastic table and chair outside the office, generally say it allows them to think more clearly and use their time more productively, with fewer unhealthy coffee or snack breaks.

▶ Does your office have the potential to be used for any other purpose? This could be important if your circumstances change in the future or if you choose to sell up. You may not have the money to put in shower facilities at this stage, for example, or be willing to lose the space, but if you keep a large upright cupboard area free of any wiring, it would be a relatively simple conversion job further down the line.

>Now you see it ... Foldaway solutions

At the other end of the spectrum, if even finding space for a desk is a real struggle, it is still possible to work from home. You do, though, have to be brutally honest with yourself about the way that you operate. Resourceful manufacturers have found stowaway solutions for almost every room in the house but they do rely on you being scrupulously tidy and, if you share your home with anyone else, in strict control of your hours. If you know from experience that you are likely to be constantly surrounded by a sea of papers and trying to make calls into the evening, you really do need a more permanent base, even if it means you have to put your homeworking plans on hold for a while.

'I moved some furniture around ... and I've made the corner furthest from the settees and television my office space'

For those ready to take up the challenge, there are a range of options available. Some kitchen companies offer units specifically designed for working there, with computer screens that flip down to protect them and free up the worksurface for other things. Hideaway cabinets can be purchased in a variety of styles and materials to blend in with your existing furniture in the sitting room or dining room,

'The office has blended beautifully and has really become a part of the garden now'

and pull-out computer tables and storage units can be set up in fitted wardrobes, landing cupboards and other closets and cubby holes. Wherever your foldaway office is sited, the important thing is that it can be put away and out of sight when you don't need it.

It worked for me...

Rachael, 44, Bristol

Rachael has worked from home for three years. She says:

'With three children at home, guests already have to sleep on a sofa bed in the lounge so I never stood a chance of getting my own separate office.

The kitchen is where everyone congregates in our house; we've got a big table in there and most visitors don't actually get any further. I didn't think it would be fair on anyone for me to claim that as my workspace and expect it to stay empty and quiet during the day. The lounge is the only other room big enough for a desk so that's where I've ended up. I moved some furniture around I've made the corner furthest from the settees and television my office space.

I put some shelves high up on the wall above the desk to keep the clutter round my feet to a minimum, and I got an old, dark wood desk and a leather executive-style chair so it would blend into the room as much as possible.

My absolute best buy has been a beautiful carved wood screen that I fell in love with in an antiques shop. My idea at the time was that I would put it up whenever I was working to help me concentrate and act as a 'Do not disturb' sign, but I quickly stopped that because it made the area quite dark and also meant I couldn't see through to where the children were after school and check everything was calm. Instead, I put it up around my office corner when I finish work for the day. It helps keep my work private but mainly it's a way of letting me relax in the evenings without constantly looking at what I've got to do in the morning or seeing that the answerphone on my business line is flashing.'

It worked for me...

Sophie, 39, south-west London

Sophie has worked from her home office for two years. She says:

'My husband and I both work from home and we shared an office in our previous property, which wasn't conducive to our relationship!

With a young family, we knew we were outgrowing our flat. We did our research and discovered that buying a three-bedroom house and building a garden office for me was a cheaper option than a four-bedroom house in London. I'm also an outdoors person and it was a bit of a dream for me to work in the garden. I employed a specialist company and the whole process was complete within a couple of months. The actual installation only took two days as the office is fully constructed elsewhere then dismantled and put back together on site. I had to get an electrician to lay the cable from the main house to the office and connect it, and a contractor to lay the foundation, both before the office arrived. The total cost, including the office itself, the cable and hook up to the pre-installed consumer unit, the foundation, and some carpentry I have subsequently had done, was in the region of £16,000. There were no planning issues as the office is not connected to the mains water supply, is at least 15ft from my house and not near the highway. It is also tiny at only 8ft x 9ft.

We have a wireless network set up and I did need to buy a booster unit for the router so that I got good wireless speeds in the office. The handheld landline from the house gets reception out there so I didn't bother connecting the phone sockets supplied with the office. I chose to have cedar cladding as it blends into the garden more and requires less maintenance than the cheaper tongue-and-groove cladding. I also hated the laminate flooring that came as standard so had a soft wood floor. I went for a non-standard cedar shingle roof too – again to look as natural as possible as

continued

our garden is quite small anyway and, having moved from a flat without a garden, we didn't want to place an eyesore in it. The office has blended beautifully and has really become a part of the garden now. We have a little fridge in there that we put wine in when we are on the adjacent patio! I love the fact that I can close the door when the working day is finished and my business doesn't encroach on family life, which it did when the office was next door to the sitting room. It's very peaceful in the garden and I really can get so much done because I'm not disturbed. Having my office completely separate from the house also means that I no longer have files, work-related post and such-like cluttering up my home. The only disadvantage is that I have no toilet, which is annoying when it's pouring with rain. I'm thinking of buying a portable chemical camping loo!'

Resources:

Useful websites

Directgov: www.direct.gov.uk – the 'Home and community' section covers planning, building regulations, choosing traders and DIY
Electrical Contractors' Association: www.eca.co.uk
Federation of Master Builders consumer site: www.findabuilder.co.uk
National Federation of Builders: www.builders.org.uk
Shedworking: www.shedworking.co.uk. An enthusiastic blog from a dedicated homeworker with links to other garden office articles and related websites and suppliers
UKPlanning: www.ukplanning.com

Further reading

▶ *Home Extensions: The Complete Handbook* by Paul Hymers (New Holland Publishers)

An easy-access book touching on everything from legal and planning issues to dealing with the professionals, this will help homeowners with a little specialist knowledge to avoid the cowboys.

▶ *Loft Conversions: Planning, Managing and Completing Your Conversion* by Laurie Williamson (The Crowood Press)

A handy starting point, covering the potential for DIY in loft conversions as well as tips for contracting out the job.

▶ *Loft Conversions* by John Coutts (WileyBlackwell)

A more technical guide, aimed at those within the trade as well as homeowners, but useful if you plan to get involved or oversee the work yourself.

▶ *Shedworking: The Alternative Office Revolution* by Alex Johnson (The Friday Project)

A quirky spin-off from www.shedworking.co.uk.

Kitting out

4

So you have chosen your office and you now need to transform it into a functional and attractive workspace. One of the joys of leaving a corporate office environment is that you can wave goodbye to synthetic carpets, fluorescent strip lighting and grey metal blinds, and inject some style and inspiration into your environment. Once you have taken care of the essentials – enough storage, good lighting and a practical layout that allows you to reach the phone from your desk and gives you empty surface space so you can have reference material and notes to hand when you need them – the rest is up to you.

If you are kitting out a home office from scratch, or going for a full makeover, the best starting point is to measure the area carefully and map it out to scale on squared paper. Mark all doors, windows, radiators, electric and phone sockets, built-in cupboards and other fixtures, so you can plan how you will furnish and arrange the room in advance. That way you can shop for your desk, filing and shelving units and any freestanding technology with a list of maximum dimensions so you don't make any expensive mistakes or have to compromise on your whole set-up because one storage cabinet doesn't quite fit where it was meant to. It sounds obvious but don't forget to factor in plenty of room for opening doors, drawers and other moving components.

Be certain at this stage that you have enough sockets in convenient locations and fit new ones if not. If you plan on decorating, any jobs like this obviously need to be done first, and a tangle of wires and extension leads looks unprofessional and is an inevitable tripping hazard. Seek advice and find registered electrical contractors in your area at www.eca.co.uk.

>The right style

The right style depends on whether the room serves a purpose other than as your office, as well as on the nature of your work and your personality. If you have a blank canvas, consider your future plans with regard to the house. Estate agents are suggesting that in some areas and types of property, a home office is more enticing to buyers than an additional bedroom. But if the décor doesn't inspire other people to imagine the room as a workspace then you could lose out on that potential selling point. Similarly, if you expect to invite clients or colleagues into your office, being too individual could give the impression of a lack of professionalism.

Unless you have been building up a picture of your ideal home office for years and already know where you are going to get everything, it can be helpful to look at as many examples as possible to get an idea of what would work for you.

▶ Home Office Snapshots (home.officesnapshots.com) is exactly what it says – an ever-expanding collection of photos posted by homeworkers. Some are more artistic than useful, and others will give you plenty of suggestions on what *not* to do, but it's still a good source of inspiration.

▶ The 'Design inspiration' section of the BBC Homes website (www.bbc.co.uk/homes) features pictures of a variety of home offices created by television design gurus for home improvement or makeover shows, including details of where you can purchase everything in them.

▶ The collaborative website www.housetohome.co.uk showcases home offices that have previously appeared in interiors magazines, categorising them according to style and again giving suppliers' information for creating the same look.

Ultimately it's about how different colours and designs make you feel, as well as how they will work in the space available to you. Does your job call for you to be creative or to focus closely on data, facts and figures? Do you need to be fired up to be productive or do you work best in a calm environment? Would a clean, contemporary, even minimalist, look help to keep you organised and efficient, or would you feel happier somewhere cosier with softer lines and a warmer, more homely feel? If you work in a visual field, as an artist, illustrator or designer, for example, remember that your office can be a showcase for your work, not just for visitors but photographed on your brochures or website. In that case, either aim to keep the background décor completely neutral so all the focus is on samples of your work on the walls or in the form of furniture or accessories, or go for a complementary style.

>The colour scheme

Your first dilemma is probably going to be what shade to paint the walls, and this is a key decision. Colours can affect your mood and levels of productivity and creativity, give a small area the illusion of spaciousness and make a workspace either distinct from the rest of a room or blend in.

If your office is located within a room that is already quite cramped, using the same light colour throughout – and, ideally, also out into the hallway or any adjoining areas – will help to open up the space. In that case, your focus with furniture and other accessories, should be on choosing styles and materials that fit with those in the rest of the room and give the whole space a cohesive look. If the room is large enough to be broken down visually into sections, painting the alcove or area where your office is sited in a coordinating but bolder, brighter shade will separate it from the living space, giving you more freedom when furnishing it and a helpful psychological delineation at the end of the day.

Similarly, homeworkers with a garden office or large windows or glass doors that open onto outdoor space often make the most of their situation by carrying the outside palette of greens, blues, off-whites and earthy tones into their workspace. This can be very successful, although paler versions tend to work much better on walls than exact matches of the natural hues, which can be dark or vivid. In general, remember the tried-and-tested rule that lighter shades make a small room more airy while deeper colours close in the walls for a cosier den.

South-facing rooms with loads of natural light can be made to look even sunnier if painted in warm shades – oranges, reds, yellows and pinks – though the effect can be somewhat overpowering in the full glare of the sun. Cool shades – blues, greens and purples – will give a lighter, airier feel. Bear in mind that very pale neutral colours may just seem washed out in strong light so you can afford to be slightly more dramatic in your choices. North-facing rooms, which tend to be colder and shadier, should be heated up with warm tones.

So what is the optimum colour for your workspace? Many people are sceptical about the power of colour to enhance or dampen your productivity in the office, but colour is used frequently in other areas of business. How many restaurants have you visited with red walls and tablecloths? Yes, it's cheerful, but beyond that it has been chosen in a lot of cases because it is believed to stimulate the appetite. There are also more aesthetic reasons for selecting or avoiding particular shades.

Red: As well as making you feel hungry (not necessarily a good thing with the kitchen so close to hand), red is invigorating and should keep you alert and driven, though it can also be tiring.

Blue: A popular choice for home offices, blue is known for its relaxing properties but is also said to encourage communication, intuition and creativity.

Green: Natural and tranquil, but some people believe it promotes hesitancy and indecision.

White: If your room is dark and gloomy, painting it dazzling white is unlikely to make it look brighter – without light, the walls will simply appear greyish.

Yellow: Sunny and lively, yellow can make you feel happy. It's welcoming in small spaces.

Orange: With the cheerful quality of yellow and the energy of red, orange can bring out both enthusiasm and a harder determination. It can make rooms feel hot, though, so is not an ideal choice if your office gets too warm anyway or already tends towards being slightly stuffy or airless.

Pink: Popular in bedrooms and bathrooms, pink induces tranquility but can also encourage passivity, so is unlikely to work for you if your job requires a bit of fire and channelled aggression.

Purple: Few people would choose to decorate an office in full-on royal purple, but lighter shades like violet and lavender are calming and can help to balance the mind.

Neutrals: Used alone, shades such as cream, khaki, sand, grey and off-white often make a room feel like the bland corporate office environment you were hoping to leave behind. Using different shades of these colours to pick out the walls, ceiling, any borders or trim, door and window frames and the adjoining area of the house will make your home flow and give the sense of a serene landscape.

Rich shades: Colours such as burgundy, chocolate and olive can have a grand executive feel, and they work very well with a wooden floor and leather or dark wood furniture. For most homes they are just a bit too imposing but if you have the property to carry the look and it fits with your professional image, it can certainly be impressive, and it might provide just the right environment to incite high-flying ambitions.

If you know what colour would suit your personality and style of working but don't think it's a physical fit for the office space available to you, keep the walls neutral and use your statement shade for furniture and furnishings instead. Or consider using it on the floor. Simple walls and boldly painted wooden floorboards or rugs can have great impact without being overwhelming.

>Good lighting

Finally, no more staring straight at a wall or abiding by an office policy of constantly closed blinds. In your home office, you can sit right in the window and know that enjoying the view is also good for you. Not only does positioning your desk that way mean any glare on your computer screen is minimised, but studies also suggest that looking onto outdoor space helps your body clock, reduces the risk of seasonal affective disorder, aids concentration and gives you room to think. If the view from your window is isn't inspiring, make a trip to the nursery right at the start – hanging plants and flowers or window boxes can work wonders.

In a home office you should be able to exploit natural light far more than most larger set-ups allow, but for additional illumination you will need task and ambient lighting options. Task lighting needs to be functional, in the

> **Definition:**
>
> **Seasonal affective disorder:**
>
> Often abbreviated – appropriately – to SAD and also referred to as the winter blues, this is a mood disorder causing depression, anxiety, irritability, a loss of energy and frequently an increased appetite and desire to sleep during the winter months. It is linked to decreased exposure to daylight and can be treated by the use of phototherapy (or light box therapy) and vitamin D supplements.

form of spotlights or anglepoise lamps with a strong beam for reading, computer work and other jobs that could otherwise put a strain on your eyes. Spotlights set into the ceiling for this purpose can look very attractive and don't take up any valuable desk space but you are obviously then restricted if you want to move furniture around in the future. Some purpose-designed computer desks come with a light bar mounted above your monitor, or you can fit something similar to the underside of shelving units on the wall. If you use a fixture of this nature, you must ensure your computer is positioned exactly as intended or you may actually create glare or shadows. Anglepoise lamps offer the greatest flexibility and can be attached to the wall if surface space is at a premium. It is worth paying extra for a good quality model as the hinges otherwise tend to weaken over time, leaving you with little control over direction. Bear in mind that some task lighting may need to be adjusted several times a day as the sun moves round and the natural light changes.

For ambient lighting, which creates atmosphere in the room, try not to rely on one overhead bulb. Downlighters cast distinct pools of light from the ceiling, where they are recessed or mounted on the surface, and can be fixed or swivel. If they don't move, they will only work well in an office if you can be sure that the layout won't change. Too many downlighters can make a place feel like a shop and they generally need to be used in conjunction with other ambient lighting to avoid overall gloominess.

Uplighters are ideal for offices because they bounce light off the ceiling, preventing glare and giving a soft look. They should be fixed at eye level or higher and work particularly well with halogen bulbs, which give a purer, whiter light than conventional ones. You will only get the desired effect if the ceiling is painted in a pale shade, though.

If you use several different areas of your office for different tasks – the desk, a larger table for spreading out paperwork and an easy chair or sofa for comfortable reading, for example – you may want to install track lighting. It is currently proving popular in home offices because it is relatively cheap and easy to install and can offer ambient and task lighting in one system. The track itself can be rather more eye-catching than you might like, and the advantages of this option are generally more about functionality and flexibility than style.

Whatever forms of ambient lighting you use, it is important that they keep the areas immediately around your task lighting sufficiently bright to avoid harsh

Interior design: Tricks of the trade

It can sometimes be hard to put your finger on exactly what it is about one room that makes it welcoming and stylish while another just doesn't quite hit the mark. Here are some inside ideas that the professionals regularly put into practice:

▶ Find your focal point. Every room should have an initial point of interest that catches the eye. It may already be there in the shape of a huge window, an impressive view or a beautiful fireplace, but if not then you should create one with a stunning piece of furniture. Don't go for anything so big or dominant that it overpowers the room, though. An open table-style desk can be ideal.

▶ Don't try to make cushions and other accessories an exact match. It will look too contrived. A mix of different shades from the same overall colour scheme will appear naturally stylish.

▶ Use the 60–30–10 rule, based on a man's suit – 60% of the look is the suit colour, 30% the shirt and 10% the tie. In your home office, the walls should be 60% of the colour in the room, a secondary colour for furniture, rugs, blinds or curtains, etc. should be 30%, and an accent colour for cushions, lamps, artwork, etc. should be the final striking 10%.

▶ Remember the ceiling when you are choosing your colour scheme, and don't just leave it white. Painting it to match the room will give you a cosy, inviting look, but the general rule is that if the walls are taller than 8ft (2.4m), the ceiling should be two shades darker and if they are less than 8ft, the ceiling should be two shades lighter.

▶ Add some black. Whether it's a lamp, a picture frame or artwork, every room can benefit from the contrast.

contrasts, which your eyes will strain to adapt to. Similarly, you should ensure that the backdrop to your monitor is well lit – another reason that sitting it in front of a window is beneficial during daylight hours.

The most likely cause of eye strain and headaches while working at your computer is glare, caused by light reflecting off the screen. If you position lights so that you cannot see the bulbs directly, this will be avoided. Alternatively you may need to reassess where to put your monitor, and invest in an anti-glare screen. For more information on safe computer use, see Chapter 7.

>Choosing office furniture

The rapid expansion of the home office market means that when it comes to buying desks, chairs, and storage and shelving units, the choices are almost limitless. Options range from complete solutions – full-size workstation, pedestal storage unit and large bookcase – for less than £150 to high-end bespoke office furniture costing thousands of pounds. Whether you want to work at a practical wipe-clean desk complete with keyboard drawer and hard-drive stand, a solid antique table or a portable glass unit that will double up as a coffee table depends on taste, space and budget. It is possible to tick all the boxes for both functionality and style, but there are several factors you should take into consideration to be sure that the set-up that looks perfect in store or on the internet will work for you in your own home.

Fully functional

It is important that your office is fully functional. It may be obvious but it won't matter how much wow factor your office exudes if you are unable to work because of back pain or you can't answer the phone without knocking a pile of paperwork to the floor because your files are already full. Bear the following in mind when looking at desks and chairs.

▶ Is the surface area of the desk really large enough for your needs?

The gradual disappearance of bulky monitors as blade PCs and laptops have taken over means few people require the vast expenses of desk space they may have done a few years ago. However, you still need enough room to position your computer, keyboard and mouse correctly. The keyboard should be directly in front of you and you shouldn't have to twist to view the monitor. You also need sufficient space to have the phone within easy reach, to be able to write as well as type freely, and to keep ongoing paperwork, pens and other frequently used equipment accessible.

▶ Is the desk height right for you or adjustable?

This is the inherent problem that many people have with using a table rather than a purpose-built desk. When you sit comfortably in your chair, your desk should be approximately at elbow level. Ideally the keyboard should be positioned slightly lower – sliding keyboard drawers do have an ergonomic purpose as well as saving space and keeping your desk area tidy when not in use. The monitor should be a little higher. There are various office accessories on the market to help you achieve the optimum set-up, but it will be considerably harder if your desk is the wrong height in the first place.

▶ Would a U or L-shaped desk arrangement allow you to reach more of what you need to without causing you to overstretch or twist?

▶ Does a desk with fitted drawers or storage still leave room for your hard drive?

Quick equipment check:

- ○ Is the surface area of the desk really large enough for your needs?
- ○ Is the desk height right for you or adjustable?
- ○ Would a U or L-shaped desk arrangement allow you to reach more of what you need to without causing you to overstretch or twist?
- ○ Does a desk with fitted drawers or storage still leave room for your hard drive?
- ○ Does your chair offer full support, adjustability and manoeuvrability?

The wires connecting the different elements of a PC don't tend to be very long, and it is important that you don't end up with the hard drive directly under the desk. If you don't have sufficient leg room, you will be uncomfortable or compromise by sitting at an angle, potentially putting strain on your back. It is also essential that the slots in the unit that allow cooling air to circulate are not blocked or the computer will overheat.

▶ Does your chair offer full support, adjustability and manoeuvrability?

You should be able to change the height of the seat and the backrest so that it follows the curve of your spine. You should also be able to alter the armrests (which ought to be padded) so your arms hang freely from your shoulders. For the majority of people it is best to buy a swivel chair to help avoid twisting the back or neck.

See Chapter 7 for more information on ergonomic office furniture and accessories, and their safe use.

Blending in

If you have a standalone office then you have free rein as far as the style of your furniture goes. Make functionality the priority though, and consider the look of the room as a whole, seeing your desk and storage choices in relation to size, features, colour scheme and lighting. As with the décor, be wary of anything too eccentric if you expect anyone else to see your workspace.

For those whose office doubles up as something else or is located within another room, the emphasis in terms

Definition:

Ergonomic:

A term and concept that really took off in the 1990s, ergonomic products – typically furniture and hand-held items – are designed with the workings of the human body in mind. As a result their shape and method of use should prove easier and more comfortable, lessening the risk of any strain or injury developing.

of style will primarily be on integration. Obviously if the room is so large that your workspace functions as a distinct area, and particularly if you have given it that identity with a different colour scheme, then you can go for a contrasting look. Otherwise your aim on the whole is to make your office blend in with the existing surroundings. That might mean a traditional, dark wood desk in the living room, pine in the kitchen or white in the bedroom. Or if the overall feel of your home is more modern and vibrant, glass and metal or bold colours in minimalist or geometric designs. Unusual materials such as bamboo make desks look less corporate so they work very well where the desk has to double up, for example, as a dressing table in a guest room.

If you have found the perfect office furniture but the full set-up you'd like is too expensive, a cheaper neutral desk or hideaway cabinet can be given an instant upgrade by replacing the standard office chair, perhaps with something more luxurious in leather or an ultra-contemporary shape and fabric. Storage units, including filing cabinets, are now available in a wide range of colours and designs so unless there's a good functional reason for choosing a corporate-style metal tower, go for something far softer-looking and more individual.

The other common intention when it comes to integrating your workspace into your home is to pack your desk area away as unobtrusively as possible at the end of the working day. Individual computer desks are compact and typically have wheels so they can be moved out of the way. Storage bins and filing cabinets on wheels are similarly flexible, and shorter towers can slide under your desk or another table. That can make it possible to tidy the whole set-up away neatly in minimal space, so it's worth taking a note of your desk height before going shopping.

The alternative is to use some form of screen to block your office area from view outside working hours. This can be a good solution if the furniture – for whatever reason – isn't stylistically a good fit with the rest of the room. It obviously works particularly well if your workspace is inset in an alcove or understairs area, for example, where you can use a simple roll-down blind to shield it, in colours and materials that coordinate with the room as a whole. Painted concertina doors can also be a functional and attractive option where suitable. Freestanding screens, whether in wood or printed fabric, have the advantage of being easily movable and can be a really striking focal point.

>If you are very short of space

However limited the space available for your home office, it is possible to make it compact rather than cramped. With specialist design consultancies estimating that around 60% of the home offices they work on would be considered small, the market is packed with ideas not only for physically reducing the space used but also for giving the impression of a bigger room.

Storage solutions

Old-fashioned metal filing cabinets often aren't the most efficient use of space. Give some thought to the storage options you need. Do you have a lot of paperwork that has to be filed away long-term, but which you will never or rarely need to refer to? If so, look for damp-proof plastic units or boxes that can be stacked elsewhere in your property. Of the papers you will require regularly, can they be easily found and accessed from a system of box or lever files that can be placed on shelves? If these are mounted on the wall above your desk, their contents are within reach but not taking up valuable space on your work surfaces or floor. For the same reason, wall-mounted bulletin boards can be the best place to keep calendars, forward planners, lists of contact details or other information that you look at several times a day.

> I also use stackable filing boxes in black and red so they can be in a square instead of a tower, which looks far less corporate

The same principles apply with storage units as with everything else – dark-coloured cabinets or boxes, especially if they form a tower or wall, will make a room feel overwhelmed and gloomy, while paler shades can help to sustain a sense of airiness. Transparent units can make the space look disorganised unless you are very neat.

Optical illusions

There are numerous tricks you can try at every stage of creating your home office to make the space appear larger than it really is.

▶ White accessories, gloss paint and light-coloured tiles and polished floors all reflect light, making a room feel more airy.

▶ If the ceiling is low, giving a sense of claustrophobia, wallpaper with thin vertical stripes in pale colours and white will make it seem higher.

▶ Choosing the same colour for the walls, shelving and office furniture such as the desk and storage unit will help to open out a tiny room.

▶ Don't be afraid to use large mirrors in a home office. Particularly if positioned on a wall directly opposite a window, they reflect lots of light, making a small space appear bigger.

▶ Bracketless shelves make walls appear cleaner and more open.

▶ Buy a glass-topped desk, which will allow light to filter underneath the furniture, giving the appearance of an open environment. Chairs with open arms have a similar effect.

▶ Set furniture at an angle so it's seen in the context of the diagonal, which is obviously the longest line in the room. This has the added advantage of potentially freeing up storage space in the corner.

▶ Don't have furniture right up against the wall or packed in without a gap between items. It might seem contradictory when every last centimetre counts, but visually those little spaces will open out the room.

>Time to call in the professionals?

If your strengths lie elsewhere and you don't know where to start with applying ideas and information, you may want to invest in the help of a specialist designer. The same is true if you plan for your office to be a real showcase for you, your work or your home, and you are looking for some professional flair to make the difference. You can find assistance whatever your budget, with some furniture chains offering expert advice, as well as the more upmarket bespoke designers who specialise in home offices. Their websites,

'I got my first desk from ... Freecycle ... [but] I did splash out on ... a good ergonomic desk chair'

catalogues and portfolios usually provide plenty of inspiration if you eventually decide to go it alone after all.

It worked for me...

Lindsay, 30, Edinburgh

Lindsay has worked from her home office in Edinburgh for six months. She says:

'The guest bedroom was the obvious choice for my home office so I sold the double bed that was in there and bought a good-quality, stylish-looking sofa bed to replace it. That left me with room for a reasonable-sized corner desk, and I managed to find one that's made up of two separate connecting parts. That's been brilliant because it means that when people come to stay I can wheel the computer table across the landing into my bedroom so I can work late at night or early in the morning without disturbing them. The other bit stays put and I stack everything underneath it and fling a throw over the top so guests have a table to use.

The room's not very big and it had been fairly recently painted white so I left that and decided to add colour with furniture and accessories instead. The look I've gone for is quite contemporary and minimalist – it's even turned out a bit space age. It's quite difference to the style of the rest of the house but because it only adjoins the landing, which is totally neutral, I don't think that matters. The desk is glass and chrome and my chair is bright red so I've put red and black-and-white patterned cushions on the white sofa bed. I've got some large black-and-white photos framed on the wall – they're just abstract images I took myself; tree branch silhouettes and real close-ups of household objects like lamps. They make the place feel more personal. I also use stackable filing boxes in black and red so they can be in a square instead of a tower, which looks far less corporate.

I wanted a stylish area to work in but I regularly have friends and relatives to stay and I really wanted them to feel relaxed and comfortable, not like they were sleeping in an office. For that reason, I've also taken the bulb out of the pendant light and use free-standing lamps, table lamps and wall-mounted spotlights so I can make the room as bright or cosy as I want to.'

It worked for me...

Danny, 36, Brighton

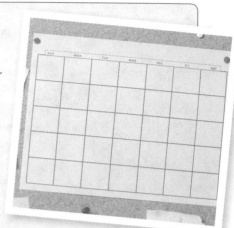

Danny has worked from his home office for two years. He says:

'Setting up your own business is expensive and when I was paying out for technology, web design, advertising and publicity material and I didn't know when the first orders were going to come in, I really didn't want to spend a lot of money on my office. I got my first desk from somebody giving it away on Freecycle, which means it didn't cost me anything except the petrol to pick it up from the other side of town. It was in good condition but it didn't have any built-in drawers or shelves so when I saw another one advertised in the local free paper for £15, I replaced it. I bought the cheapest possible open shelving units from a furniture chainstore, but they look fine once they're covered in books and filing boxes. I also got basic plastic storage boxes with lids for paperwork like old invoices that I have to keep for legal and tax reasons but don't need regular access to. The one thing I did splash out on was a good ergonomic desk chair with adjustable lumber support because I've had problems with my back in the past.

I've left the décor exactly as it was for the time being, but almost covered two walls with big, cheap cork notice boards. I pin everything on them from to-do lists and phone numbers to designs in progress and pictures of finished work for inspiration. It means I can see everything I need instantly and look at alternative designs side by side to compare, plus it makes the room look far more colourful and interesting.'

Resources:

Useful websites

BBC Homes: www.bbc.co.uk/homes
Dulux: www.dulux.co.uk – a commercial site, but it offers a variety of interactive tools for choosing colours, creating mood boards and trying out combinations
Freecycle: www.freecycle.org
Housetohome: www.housetohome.co.uk

Further reading

▶ *Ideas for Great Home Decorating* (Sunset)

A comprehensive guide covering everything from colours and textures to flooring and lighting, and how to create a cohesive style.

▶ *Storage: Get Organised* by Terence Conran (Conran Octopus)

Practical information and creative inspiration for organising every area of your home.

▶ *The Sunday Times Small Spaces for Modern Living; Making the Most of Your Indoor Space* by Caroline Atkins (Hamlyn)

An in-depth look at maximising the space available to you using principles of design and colour, clever lighting and storage solutions and the right furniture.

Equipping yourself

5

MFP, LCD, RAM, PDA. If you aren't technically minded, IT can look like a minefield of meaningless jargon. Suddenly being responsible for installing, using and maintaining your own equipment can be one of the most intimidating aspects of becoming a homeworker. Fortunately, you don't have to become a computer whizz. As long as you know where to turn for expert advice and help if needed, and have enough knowledge to make informed decisions about what to buy, which systems to use and when to get the professionals on board, then you are all set.

There is a lot of talk currently about technology being future-proof, and it's true that the market, particularly within the communications sector, has been undergoing rapid change and will continue to do so. But only a very small minority of people will need equipment that is teetering on the cutting edge. For most, the real issues are functionality and cost. And fortunately both of those are becoming more and more attuned to the needs of homeworkers. Unlike the situation just a few years ago, there is now a huge amount on the market that is aimed at those who work from home or while they are on the move. Teleworkers are no longer peripheral but the target of some of the biggest brands in technology. There are whole ranges designed to be suitable for every level of home office use, so you can compare price, capabilities, size and security, and choose exactly what's right for you.

>Choosing a computer

Unless there's a reason not to, it makes sense to buy a machine that is at least similar in make and model to the one you had in the office. That way finding and using everything will be

automatic and you won't waste time discovering a new computer's idiosyncracies. It also means that if you are continuing to work for your old employer, all the programs will be compatible and if you run into difficulties, the IT department should be able to talk you through solving them. Having said that, because all the major PC software is close to universal, you will probably only experience problems with compatibility if you opt for a Mac when the main office operates PCs or vice versa. In practice, this rarely happens because the decision between a PC and a Mac tends to effectively be made for you by the nature of your work. Companies that work in publishing, graphic or web design, advertising, printing and other arts are typically standardised on the Mac. Everyone else uses Windows.

The following sections describe what your other main considerations should be.

Processor speed

The brand of processor has no effect on the hardware or software you can use or, indeed, on anything but the number of applications you will be able to run at any one time and the speed at which the computer will react when using them. You only need to pay for a faster processor if you will be dealing with large datasets in spreadsheets or editing graphics and similar. A low-speed processor will be sufficient for normal word processing, and internet and email use.

RAM

RAM (random access memory) is the temporary storage space used by applications and the operating system when your PC is running. Again, if your requirements are limited to basic web browsing, work processing and email, you probably won't need more than 256MB of RAM, although most computers now come with a minimum of 512MB as standard. If you are working with a lot of digital photos, graphics or videos, 1GB is almost essential and 2GB could come in handy.

Hard drive

This is the permanent home of the machine's operating system, installed applications and your saved files. The first two will generally use up to 10GB of the available space, so how much you need is dependent entirely on what you intend to save. Hard drives range in size from a now rarely seen 40GB to around 500GB. If you are storing only word-processing documents and spreadsheets, you will be looking right at the low end of the scale, but if you need to keep large numbers of digital photos and, particularly, video files, then the rule of thumb is the bigger the better. Bear in mind that the greatest consumers of hard drive space tend to be MP3 files, camcorder footage and similar – so it may be your leisure use and that of your family rather than your work requirements that you have to accommodate.

Monitor

To the relief of most space-strapped homeworkers, bulky old-style monitors have been largely replaced by LCD or flat panel screens. These tend to be fairly high resolution, creating a clearer, sharper picture that will help to reduce eye strain. They also minimise reflective glare. The standard size is 17 in but if you are working with graphics applications or need to use a large font, you may want to opt for a 19 in or 21 in model instead. Many monitors are sold with inbuilt speakers but the quality tends to be relatively poor. Unless you will only want sound infrequently, experts generally suggest that you buy separate speakers to meet your requirements.

Keyboard and mouse

Your choice will be restricted by the type of connection on the motherboard, but beyond that it is a matter of personal preference. If you will be spending a lot of time typing or using the mouse it's worth looking at ergonomic designs, intended to reduce the risk of repetitive strain injury.

>Laptops and PDAs

Definition:

PDA:

The PDA (personal digital assistant) is most commonly known by the ubiquitous brand name BlackBerry. Effectively a hand-held computer, the original models offered a calendar, to-do list, contacts database and note-taker, but wireless capabilities now mean internet access and email services come as standard, and many PDAs also double up as a mobile phone. They are used with a mini keyboard and scroll wheel, or a stylus and touch-screen technology, or both.

Does the nature of your job mean you will spend a considerable amount of time away from home, either travelling to and from meetings or for more extended periods? Will you need access to your email, applications and files while you are there? Alternatively, are you only working from home one or two days a week and spending the rest of the time in the office, perhaps hot-desking? If so, then a laptop or PDA could be essential. Experts recommend that you don't use a laptop as a main computer, partly because the screen size is generally smaller than your eyes will find comfortable, but mainly because the height and angle will encourage poor, slumped posture and put strain on your back and neck. This can be alleviated with the use of an adjustable riser, but when setting up your home office it is best to think of a laptop as supplementary to your PC. Indeed, with the rise and rise of PDAs, you may not need one at all, even if you spend a lot of time on the road.

A PDA has the advantage of fitting into your pocket or an existing bag and many also double up as a mobile phone. They are ideal for checking emails and referring to documents, schedules and contacts, but their size obviously makes them impractical if you will have large amounts of typing to do. The keyboards can be very fiddly so you may prefer to choose one with a stylus – experiment with that you find easiest and quickest to use before buying. You will also be unable to load the full range of office software on a PDA that you can on a laptop.

Whichever option you are going for, check in advance that it will allow you to do everything you need to do while away from the office, and that it will be fully compatible with your main PC. Also ask about security features because mobile devices are by their very nature more vulnerable to theft. Choosing a laptop calls for many of the same considerations as buying your main computer, but you will also want to look at weight, battery capacity for when you don't have access to a mains socket, multiple USB ports if you need to connect more peripherals and wireless capability.

>Printer or MFD?

A printer is the second most common piece of office equipment to be found in private homes, with a large number of people buying them purely for leisure use. As e-tickets and online payments and receipts for everything become more popular, they are increasingly valuable in daily life. As a growing number of people are using digital cameras and preferring to print their own pictures, there is a burgeoning market for machines combining high quality results with compact, easy to use design.

If your work printing requirements are fairly basic and the quantities likely to be light to moderate, a model suitable for domestic use may well be all you need. Before you consider the exact specifications, however, you have to decide whether you require

> **Definition:**
>
> **MFD:**
> Also referred to as an MFP (multifunction product or peripheral) or all-in-one, an MFD (multifunction device) combines a printer, scanner, photocopier and sometimes a fax in one machine. Designed to save space and money, they have been targeted specifically at the SoHo (small office/home office) market.

other functions such as the ability to scan, photocopy and fax, and if a single machine combining some or all of these facilities is the best option for your home office. The most obvious advantage is size – most MFDs for the home office market aren't much bigger than desktop printers, and having one machine instead of three or four can make a huge difference when space is at a premium. A single machine will also use less energy, and the initial outlay is smaller. There was a feeling when MFDs first came into the marketplace that the quality of each individual function was reduced, but that is no longer the case. All in all, unless you require very high-end specialist equipment for printing or scanning, there is unlikely to be any advantage in buying separate machines.

Whether you opt for an MFD or decide you really only need a printer, you'll be confronted by two fundamental choices: laser or inkjet and colour or monochrome.

Laser versus inkjet

Chances are that if you have had a printer at home in the past, it has been inkjet. Traditionally, the more expensive laser machines – known for their speed but conventionally not providing the same colour quality as inkjets – belonged in larger, corporate offices where volume is all-important. The basic technical difference is that an inkjet printer releases tiny droplets of ink to form the finished image while a laser drops toner powder granules onto the paper and creates the finished image by applying heat to the area of imprint.

Which is best for you, your job and your budget will be dictated largely by the amount of printing you expect to do. You should look at your predicted volumes over the next two or three years alongside the cartridge yields of the brands you are considering and estimate an overall cost. The results may be surprising. Inkjet cartridges can cost as little as £6 or £7 and are rarely more than £25, but they will print fewer pages – particularly when you are looking at a higher density coverage, as with lots of images or graphics rather than text – than laser toners. They also have a life span that is unrelated to the number of pages they print because liquid ink will dry out within two to five years once the seal has been broken and the cartridge installed. In practice, this means that if you only do an annual colour print run – for the Christmas market, for example – you may be throwing money away. Dry laser toners, on the other hand, typically cost upwards of £75 each and some brands are priced at more than £100. They can churn out more pages, though, and will last until they have been entirely used for printing, even if the machine isn't switched on for several months.

Make sure you look at the specific details of the model you are considering because discrepancies can be huge. Particularly with inkjet printers and MFDs, the factor to watch out for is the cost of the consumables – some manufacturers implement what is known as the Gillette model, in reference to the razor blades that can be more expensive than the razor itself but without which the original product is unusable.

Colour versus monochrome

This obviously depends entirely on what you intend to print. If you are just generating hard copies of documentation for your files and other paperwork for your own annotation or reference, then black and white will be perfectly sufficient. If you are also printing letters, contracts and invoices to send to clients then you need to compare the cost of printing in colour to printing in black and white but paying extra for a supply of paper with your letterhead or logo in full colour. If you plan to create your own marketing material, mail-outs or portfolio, colour is a must. Psychologists have suggested that colour impression can account for 60% of the acceptance or rejection of any product or service, and surveys indicate that people are 55% more likely to reach for a colourful flier than one in black and white.

Until relatively recently, colour laser printers were the preserve of larger office set-ups, where it was common to have monochrome machines for everyday use and one special one for projects where colour was essential. They were generally considered to be prohibitively expensive for most home use. In the past few years, however, the purchase and servicing costs of a colour printer have dropped by an average 40%–50%. In that time, inkjet colour printers have also increased in capability and can handle far larger print jobs while retaining the quality of the results. Now, as long as the model has a monochrome printing option so the use of colour ink or toner is strictly controlled, meaning for most homeworkers a colour printer is a worthwhile investment.

Other considerations

▶ If you plan to print large numbers of photographs, you should weigh up the purchase and running costs of laser printers that are specifically designed to cope with very high-quality imagery (inevitably, these will tend to be at the top end of the market) and photo ink for inkjet printers. The difference between photo ink and ordinary colour ink is that photo ink spreads more when it hits paper, filling in the dots and getting rid of graininess. The photo inks also come in different shades and may be up to twice the price for a similar volume.

▶ Check in advance whether your printer can be used only with cartridges made by the same manufacturer. Consumables from a third party don't always provide the same quality and durability as the brand versions, but they can be significantly cheaper. Be careful, though – some printer manufacturers may only value the warranty on the machine if it uses their own cartridges.

▶ It's not just the price of ink or toner that adds up; look into the ongoing costs of other consumables including drums, maintenance and paper. Some papers – designed for both inkjet and laser printers – are especially lightweight with faster drying times, specifically intended for high-volume brochure and flyer printing. But again, some paper works better with certain printer makes and models.

▶ Most print jobs are fewer than six pages long, so you will quickly get frustrated with a machine that takes an age to warm up and start every time. Check the First Copy Out Time (FCOT) before you buy, or look for a device with zero warm-up time. This is particularly important for homeworkers, who will probably be more aware of the financial and environmental costs of leaving a printer continually on standby than people in a larger office.

▶ Find out how to employ inbuilt energy-saving modes and ask about the consumption when these are on as well as when the machine is in use or on standby.

▶ The capacity for duplex (double-sided) printing will allow you to save a lot of paper and do your bit for the environment.

▶ Ensure it is easy to switch between colour and mono printing, and have all your default settings set to black and white to deal with routine tasks.

▶ You won't have a store room full of ink or toner cartridges at your disposal so look for a machine that gives you a clear warning when the consumables are running out.

▶ Make sure that the printer or MFD has individual ink cartridges so only the colour that has run out is replaced.

▶ Some printers only feed on certain sizes, stocks or weights of paper. Ask for details of any restrictions before you buy.

▶ Look at whether the printer feeds from a bottom tray, from the back, or if it 'gravity' feeds down and out. This may not sound important but you obviously need access to refill it with paper and clear any jams, and that can affect where you are able to site the machine in a cramped office.

▶ Ask about noise levels as these can vary greatly and you will be acutely aware of sound in an otherwise quiet house.

▶ Don't overlook the other functions on an MFD. Check the speed of the modem on the fax; the optimum is 33.3kbps. Higher speeds will help to reduce your phone costs.

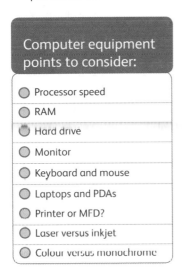

Computer equipment points to consider:

- ○ Processor speed
- ○ RAM
- ○ Hard drive
- ○ Monitor
- ○ Keyboard and mouse
- ○ Laptops and PDAs
- ○ Printer or MFD?
- ○ Laser versus inkjet
- ○ Colour versus monochrome

>Getting online

For most homeworkers broadband is essential. Unfortunately a few remote areas of the UK still don't have that option without paying out for a costly satellite connection (see Chapter 9). For the providers it's a hugely competitive market and there are many different options and packages on offer. Bearing that in mind, it's probably a mistake to tie yourself into a very long-term contract; instead keep an eye on availability and comparison websites such as www.broadbandchoices. co.uk, www.uswitch.com, www.broadband.co.uk and www.broadbandchecker. co.uk. Don't be afraid to change providers if you find a deal that will give you significant savings while still meeting all your requirements. There are horror stories about people left offline for weeks on end after trying to switch, but for the vast majority it's a very straightforward process. Bear in mind, though, that it may be a greater hassle if you have a combined package covering your phone and broadband. These can really reduce your bills, but 'encouraging' customer loyalty is obviously one of the main reasons they are offered. Run through this checklist of the most important things to consider before signing up with a new provider.

▶ Know your limits. According to a recent survey, 71% of broadband users think their package includes unlimited downloads, but 75% of deals available actually have restrictions imposed. If you persistently go over your limit, you will either be charged (typically around £2 per GB) for the excess, automatically upgraded to a more expensive monthly deal, or your provider may deliberately slow down your connection to curb your downloads. At a crucial deadline time, this could be disastrous. Look carefully at the terms of your fair usage policy to see what action could be taken and if you are aware of being a heavy user – which is quite likely if you are connecting remotely to the main office – use a free online downloads monitor to keep track.

▶ An ADSL modem will almost certainly be included in your deal, though some providers do charge for postage. While some will also give you a wireless router with a wireless broadband package, with others you will need to buy one separately. Even a top-of-the-range router will set you back less than £100 and you can pay half that, so don't be tempted to sign up with an expensive provider to get the free hardware – it will cost you more in the long run.

▶ Many people simply can't do their job without internet or email access, so check exactly what the situation will be if you run into technical problems with your broadband connection. You need to know the opening times of support lines and their costs, which can vary and easily change a cheap deal to an expensive one if you are kept on the line for long periods. Be aware of the usual tricks – it's not much help if the customer service line is free or on a local rate but most problems can only be dealt with by technical support at 50p a minute.

▶ Go through all the small print in advance if you are thinking of moving house within the period of your contract. You may have to pay to get set up again, even if you are not changing your provider, or even cover the remainder of the contract at your old address.

▶ Check out any free broadband offers. An increasing number of companies are giving away broadband connection with specific landline, mobile phone or even satellite television packages, and these can be great value if you'd have been paying for the other service anyway. However, there have been several well-publicised issues including long contracts and poor service. Some of the providers giving free broadband fare consistently badly in customer satisfaction surveys.

Why go wireless?

The advantages of opting for wireless internet connection with a router at home are the fact that you can use it from any room or area of the property, the ability to connect with more than one computer at a time, and, most obviously, the physical lack of wires. As such, it is most useful for those who have other family or household members with their own PCs or laptops, and those who have garden offices or garage conversions but may also want to work in the main house at times. The potential downsides are that it can be easier to lose the connection, there is still some scientific debate about whether the waves involved might be harmful, and there are security – and speed – implications, with other computer users in the neighbourhood able to ride along on your paid-for broadband if it's not sufficiently password-protected.

>Keeping in contact

Phone lines

Buying a combined package of broadband and landline telephone will almost certainly prove cheaper than paying for separate contracts, as long as both elements meet your needs. Whether you want a designated business line will depend on whom you share the house with, the hours they are at home and how heavy you anticipate your phone usage being. A second line will also allow you to switch off at the end of the working day. Clients and other contacts, particularly those based in another time zone may well phone at 3am your time expecting to leave a message and be surprised to have their call answered by a very sleepy or startled voice.

An 0845 local rate number or 0870 national rate number can be extremely cheap and you can normally divert these numbers to any phone. They allow you to keep your geographical location a secret, though that may actually lose you local custom. People are also often put off by 08 numbers, as by mobiles, because they don't know how much the call will cost them.

Give some thought to the phone set too. You will almost definitely want a user ID screen so you can make an informed decision about which calls to answer when you are under pressure or outside working hours. A cordless phone will give you far greater freedom to get on with other basic tasks while making calls, and if you will need your hands for typing while using the phone, you also need to ensure it is compatible with a suitable headset.

VoIP (Voice over internet protocol)

You don't have to pay for a second line for a dedicated business number. Consider using a VoIP phone, which utilises your broadband internet connection instead. As with any phone or internet contract, the terms vary considerably, but typically calls to any other VoIP number will be free and you can either pay a pre-set monthly rate for unlimited calls to UK landlines or they, and calls to mobiles, will be offered at a discounted rate – usually at least 30% less than you would pay with a conventional phone. In the past, problems with unclear or unreliable connections meant many people didn't want to use VoIP for work. But these problems have on the whole been eliminated or drastically reduced. All you need is a headset with a microphone, and many providers will set you up with a free trial.

Webcams

Although webcams are more often bought for personal use, particularly during instant messaging or VoIP conversation with distant friends or relatives, don't overlook the potential for using a webcam for work. Videoconferencing requires a level of specialism that few home offices can supply so employers and business owners will usually pay to use external facilities when this is called for. However, if you simply want to show a colleague or other contact something that cannot be easily emailed, a basic webcam can be very useful.

>Software

If you are an employee, as a general rule you just need to discuss your software requirements with your manager and the IT department at your company and ensure everything is fully compatible. If you are self-employed, you can choose from a vast range of software to take control of as much or as little of your admin as you wish. Everything from customer history and supplier details to your accounts and cash flow can be managed via your computer, and software specifically tailored to small or home-based businesses is a growing market. Not everybody needs it, however, and you should ask yourself some questions before spending what could add up to a lot of money.

Checklist:

○ Is the software compatible with my computer?

○ Will it be able to interact with any of my other software programs? Or will I need a bridge (a way to link different applications)?

○ Is it easy to install and use without IT support?

○ Will it be able to keep up with my needs in the future?

○ If I collaborate with other people or take on employees, will they also be able to use it?

○ Do I need a specific program (just for accounts, for example) or a total package? Will I be paying for more features than I need?

○ Do I need to buy software or can I download it for free? The most secure source for free software is the Open Source Initiative (www.opensource.org); for a free-to-download accounting program, visit www.turbocashuk.com.

>Security

Give a moment's thought to what you have – or will have – stored on your home office computer: your accounts; sensitive emails and confidential company information; private contact details for clients? Yet experts warn that many homeworkers may as well be printing it all out and leaving it at the local coffee shop for any stranger to peruse. More than 20% of small businesses in the UK have been subject to an online security breach. Teleworkers may be particularly vulnerable if they are lulled into a false sense of security by being an employee of a larger company when, in fact, because they are working from an external location, they are outside the business security perimeter. And if you only work from home part-time, you could also be responsible for corrupting the entire office network. A rogue virus downloaded unwittingly from a website used via an internet port at home has the potential to infiltrate the whole network

once the laptop is connected back up at the office, causing an endless list of problems.

If you have been used to working on a company-owned computer in an office, it can be a shock to have to pay for anti-virus software – and to discover how much responsibility you need to take for maintaining and updating it. Protective software scans the hard drive for viruses, either deleting them or quarantining them to a secure vault. Viruses can slow down your computer, delete important files and cause your machine to behave erratically, shutting down without warning, for example.

Various internet service providers now offer anti-virus protection bundled with their products. These are usually from leading names but do check the terms and compare the cost of purchasing anti-virus software separately in relation to your requirements before signing up to a more expensive broadband package. Bear in mind that heavy-duty software uses a lot of RAM and may slow down your system.

Unless your use of and reliance on technology is very small, anti-virus software is probably an outlay you can't avoid. Some very basic versions are available for free download, while if you go to the websites for others, you can sometimes run a free scan or check. Bear in mind that once your chosen anti-virus software is in place, you should be updating it at least once a month. Some can be set to auto-update, but at least ensure it will automatically notify you when an update is due.

A firewall is another must-have protective layer. These permit or deny things to be sent to and from a computer, stopping potential threats before the anti-virus software has to take effect. Some applications do come with their own firewall but they are not necessarily the best available so it may be worth paying extra to strengthen your defences. On the other hand, you should be able to find efficient if not absolutely top-of-the-range anti-spyware for free. Using more than one in combination will up the level of protection. Spyware is often aimed at key-logging in an attempt to see which keys are pressed when you log on to secure sites, thus allowing a hacker to decipher your passwords. More innocent, if highly irritating and equally sophisticated, spyware can identify the websites you visit on a regular basis, and bombard you with targeted pop-up advertisements on the back of that information.

In addition to installing protective software, you obviously need to take sensible precautions such as not using unsecured Wi-Fi hotspots if you are working on the move and giving your wireless connection at home a password (using names, dates and real words for this makes you an easy target but the majority of people still fall into that trap). For further advice about online security, see the section on protecting your PC at the government-sponsored website www.getsafeonline.org.

>Back-up

It may not be the first thing you want to think about when you have just finished creating and kitting out your office, but what would happen if your home fell victim to fire, flooding or any other natural or man-made disaster? Or if your computer was stolen or irreparably damaged? Obviously your insurance should cover the replacement of all your technology and perhaps some of your lost earnings too, but would vital work databases and information have been destroyed for good? When you work in a shared office, you don't have to think about backing up because it should be done for you automatically, but even if you remain an employee, as a homeworker the responsibility may well lie with you.

If paperwork and digital documentation is only a small part of your business, you may be able to back up manually by saving everything onto CDs, DVDs, USBs or a second hard-drive on a regular basis. Otherwise, there are a growing number of software packages and external online services that can do it for you. You can buy data duplication software that will track what data is changing and replicate it automatically, thus creating a snapshot in a repository, ideally located off-site. An online set-up will also save everything automatically to a digital vault. Do be aware, though, that some homeworkers have experienced problems with these automatic systems. They can be too thorough and save so many drafts, recovered versions and other unwanted documents that it can be hard to access what you are looking for when you want it.

Looking after your technology

▶ When deciding on the location of your office equipment within your home, bear in mind that technology can be vulnerable to smoke, humidity, dust and extremes of temperature. Try to avoid placing machines directly in front of radiators. Buy covers to protect the main items when not in use.

▶ Remember that air must be able to circulate freely around your computer to prevent it from overheating. Watch out for things accumulating under or around your desk and never let the ventilation slots become blocked.

▶ There is a risk that static from carpet could damage a computer's circuits, so if you must position your machine on a carpeted floor, consider buying an anti-static mat or using an anti-static spray to reduce build-up.

▶ Clean all machines regularly with specialist preparations or other recommended substances. Always apply liquids onto a cloth, never directly onto a computer, printer or keyboard.

▶ Unless it is frozen and you have no other option, never turn your computer off at the power switch or the wall. Close all the applications and shut it down systematically.

▶ Never unplug peripherals such as your printer and keyboard from the computer while it is running.

If you decide to go down the more traditional route, your duplicate copies should obviously be stored in a completely separate location, but one where you can get at them easily should the worst happen. It is also a good idea to devise a plan in case back-up data files are destroyed, because clearly remote servers can also be vulnerable to corruption through viruses. Depending on the value or sensitivity of the data you are saving, it may be worth encrypting it. This can usually be done by inserting a key – which holds the encryption – into the hard drive before transferring data. The data will then not be readable without the key, which again is stored in a different location.

> 'I then bought the specialist magazines, read the reviews and asked friends and contacts for recommendations, so I had a much better idea of what I wanted.'

When you need help

If you need help to set up your computer equipment, there are companies that will send round a team of IT wizards who will connect everything, ensure it's all working and sort out any teething problems. It won't always be necessary and will add to your costs, but if you are liable to spend several days phoning premium-rate helplines for each machine, then it could well be worth it.

Do check what support is available with a new computer, printer, MFD or broadband package at the time of purchase. Ask specifically whether the technical support line is free or what the phone charges are, and find out what length of warranty comes with the product. This is typically a year and can be extended for an additional fee, but most experts advise against doing this as your consumer rights should cover most of the same things at no cost.

It worked for me...

Marcus, 37, Lincoln

Marcus has worked from home for two years. He says:

'I bought my first printer very cheaply from a supermarket – basically because I hadn't got round to researching the market to choose the right one and it was the only place open when I urgently needed to print something. It lasted less than two months before I replaced it. It still worked fine, but it was full colour with no option for printing in black and white, the ink cartridges that came with it were empty within a fortnight, and to replace them only cost just over £5 less than buying another identical printer, which didn't seem right.

I then bought the specialist magazines, read the reviews and asked friends and contacts for recommendations, so I had a much better idea of what I wanted. I also looked into how some of the manufacturers had been rated by environmental organisations. In the end I went for a brand that advertised its system for taking back and reusing or recycling used cartridges, and I chose a model with duplex printing so I get through a lot less paper.

I would have looked at MFDs if someone hadn't already given me a scanner. It's not a particularly expensive one but it's been invaluable and means my old fax machine is now just getting dusty in the corner. I didn't receive many faxes anyway because almost everything was done by email, and when I sent them I always seemed to have problems with busy lines, pages missing or them not being received at all. I've had no issues with scanning and emailing, most of my clients seem to prefer being sent documents that way, and if there ever is a query, they're saved in my outbox with all the details.'

It worked for me...

Richard, 58, Peterborough

Richard has worked from home for 12 years. He says:

'When I first started working from home, I had the fax set up in the dining room because I only had room for my PC – which was a vast beige thing that now looks like it should be in a museum – and printer in my office. When I needed to photocopy anything, I used to go to the local library and pay per sheet.

I also spent a small fortune getting all my brochures and reports done at a professional printers so the graphics and photos were a decent quality. It was incredibly time-consuming too, but now I get pretty much instant results, that aren't noticeably different, with my own MFP. I do still outsource a couple of things, but they've changed over the years. I'm now able to use the money I save by producing my own literature for things like website design, which I can't really do myself – or not to the level I want.

I've also invested in some fairly hardcore security software after a scare a couple of years ago when it looked like a virus had wiped everything off my hard drive. Fortunately a specialist was able to recover it but I'm now religious about updating all my security programs, and I've put a proper back-up system in place. I used to periodically save all my documents onto disks, but I kept them in the storage units in my office. Someone pointed out that they wouldn't be much use to me if we had a fire, so I now keep one set on my property but in a separate building, and another with a friend – and I store his for him in return. It's worked well for us but I don't get the time to save everything as often as I'd like and I'm looking into signing up to an automatic online service.'

Resources:

Useful websites

▶ Consumer Direct: www.consumerdirect.gov.uk

▶ Get Safe Online: www.getsafeonline.org

▶ IT Professionals directory: www.itprofessionals.co.uk

▶ PC Advisor: www.pcadvisor.co.uk

Further reading

▶ *Computer Troubleshooting Manual: The Complete Step-by-Step Guide* by Kyle MacRae (Haynes)

Aimed at computer users of all levels, this covers precautionary measures and disaster recovery as well as an extensive list of common hardware and Windows problems.

▶ *The Healthy PC: Preventive Care and Home Remedies for Your Computer* by Carey Holzman (McGraw-Hill Osborne)

A beginner's guide to all things PC from routine maintenance to software management, security, the internet and downloads.

▶ *Laptop Manual: Buying, Using and Maintaining a Laptop* by Gary Marshall (Haynes)

A very accessible look at when a laptop is the right choice, what its limitations are and how to choose and use the right machine for you.

Achieving the work-life balance

6

First, the bad news. The UK has a reputation for long working hours, particularly in comparison with other European countries. Anecdotal evidence also suggests that homeworkers tend to put in longer hours than they did in the office. Since the government signed up to the EU's European Social Chapter in the late 1990s, several family-friendly, flexible working measures have been introduced – but in that same period the proportion of people working long hours (more than 48 per week) has risen from one in 10 to well over one in four.

There are several possible reasons for this. With attitudes towards homeworking still sceptical in some industries and individual companies, there is a danger of overcompensation and workers regularly going that extra mile to prove a doubting boss wrong. The traditional homeworkers' downfall of domestic interruptions and procrastination is a major contributing factor in a lot of cases and, on the other side of the coin, those with workaholic leanings will have free rein to be putting the final touches to projects until 3am in a way they may not have done in the office. A more positive explanation is that homeworkers are frequently entrepreneurs, setting up their own small businesses, and the launch of a company almost inevitably brings a period of very intense activity with evenings and weekends often sacrificed.

Clearly you will know before you even start working from home where your own strengths and weaknesses lie. If you are a perfectionist and poor delegator who is rarely able to say no then you are almost certainly going to find yourself a prisoner in your own home office. If you struggle to apply yourself to your job even with your boss looking over your shoulder, you are unlikely to be a harder taskmaster when left to your own devices. Ultimately, the home environment doesn't suit everyone. Some people do miss the interaction with colleagues and motivation from managers, and find they simply don't function well without them.

The good news, however, is that for most homeworkers it is just a matter of learning to instil the discipline and drive they may previously have got from others. It is as much about ensuring that you give yourself the breaks, leisure time and hours out of the house that you need as it is about knuckling down to work. People who say they sit for hours at their desk without moving or speaking to anybody and lose all track of time – and it is worryingly common – clearly aren't doing their health or productivity any favours. And the chances are that when they finally do shut down the computer they're going to feel pretty isolated and unhappy too. Pre-empt these problems and it is perfectly possible to avoid them altogether. After all, an entire industry has built up around advising people how to better manage their time, prioritise their tasks, escape distractions and operate more efficiently, so there are plenty of tried-and-tested techniques for homeworkers to take away.

If you are aware that your working hours are building up but are tempted to just grit your teeth and accept it as a trade-off for being at home, don't! Allowing your job to regularly infringe on your personal time will have an impact not only on your family, social life and health (less stress and greater opportunity for relaxation being among the top reasons for choosing to work from home in the first place) but also your finances. Think about your salary or the hourly value you put on your expertise if you are self-employed, and then input your genuine working hours into the calculator at www.worksmart.org.uk/workyourproperhoursday to get your true rates. It may just inspire you into taking action.

>Get organised

There are several things you can do before you even become a regular homeworker to help maximise your efficiency from the start. One of the most important is to reassess your expectations. Be realistic about the time available to you. Many new homeworkers make the mistake of thinking that without the commute, endless staff meetings and constant distractions from colleagues around them, fitting everything into the working day will be a breeze. What they often overlook is that by leaving the larger office set-up, they are losing support services such as IT and cleaning. If they have gone self-employed, that extends to areas such as human resources and publicity too. Even if you are planning on outsourcing these aspects of your business, it still takes time to organise and oversee it all. If you plan your working day or week without putting these factors into the equation then your whole routine will be thrown the moment an issue arises that needs your attention.

Get your systems in place in advance. It's all about having a structure that tasks naturally slot into so you are not wasting time searching for documents on the computer, trying to decide where to file new paperwork or typing out the same basic letter or email for the umpteenth time. Make definite decisions about things like filing systems, both paper and computerised, and accounts and invoicing – and keep them simple. Be ruthless about what you are bothering to keep – up to 85% of the documents retained by any organisation will never be looked at again. Invest in software right from the beginning if you are confident it will help to streamline your processes. Buy an organiser add-on for your email account that will automatically sort your incoming messages into virtual folders. Most will allow you to file them under date, name or company name, and categorise them according to whether they are being saved for future reference, are on your to-do list or are part of the job you are engaged in right now. Some also provide a faster, more efficient search facility than the generally laborious ones that come as standard.

If possible, decide before you start producing business cards or marketing literature whether you are going to need a separate phone line or email address for work. In most cases, they will allow you to make informed decisions about which calls to accept, and prevent you wasting work time on personal or domestic issues. If your contact details are already established, at least open a free email account and give that address to your friends, family and all the airlines, shops and others that will send you endless details of their latest offers. Similarly if you add a business name to your postal address, you won't spend half the morning filtering the mail but can instantly divide it into two piles. Having a system in place that separates work communications from any others puts the onus back on you to decide when to deal with personal correspondence and calls, rather than mixing your home life and job haphazardly throughout the day.

>Structuring your day

The real secret of good time management is simply self-discipline. No one can make you get up in the morning or stop you lingering with the paper over breakfast, but the faster you get into a pattern, the more quickly it will become habit and the easier it will get. If you know late starts are likely to be your downfall, arrange client phone calls or something similar for 9am every day for the first two weeks – and then every Monday to set up your week as you want it to continue.

Be equally rigid about your lunch break and finishing time. Parents who have to leave the house at 3pm on the dot for the school run are often the most efficient homeworkers of all because the clock's ticking and they can't mentally give themselves any leeway. Again, it can help to make early-evening arrangements until you get into a routine. Otherwise, without the motivation of a train to catch, you are likely to fall into the 'just another 10 minutes' trap and still be at your desk at 8pm. Experts say that creating an immovable stopping time is a psychological trick that will help you to concentrate harder over the hours you have available to work. A definite lunch hour will also focus your mind in the morning and give you a chance to relax so that you have more energy going into the afternoon. Just make sure you get away from your desk entirely – lunch is not the time to be sending personal emails or surfing the internet because, physically and mentally, you need a break from the computer to be productive. Think back to school with its clearly delineated periods of work and play; your days were much more concentrated and seemed longer and a great deal was achieved in what was a comparatively short time.

There will always be times when you do have to work late, make international business calls after dinner or get up at 5am to have a report waiting in someone's inbox at 9am. However, you will undo all your good work in structuring your work hours if you regularly return to your desk after you have logged off for the day. Having access to your emails 24/7 is dangerous. BlackBerry addiction is now a recognised phenomenon and homeworkers are at risk of the desktop version. If you have a separate office or work in the garden then it's obviously easier just to close the door, ideally lock it, and walk away, but if you can see your monitor from where you are watching television, it's too tempting just to check whether that important deal has come in or if you have got that feedback you have been waiting for. However, it's important for your family life, the harmony of your household and your long-term health and productivity that you don't succumb.

If you can physically hide your workspace with a pull-down blind or screen, do. If not, put your paperwork out of sight and unplug your computer at the wall. Buy a monitor cover, which has the added advantage of preventing your equipment from becoming dusty. If you use your work PC for leisure in the evenings, have a different sign-in so you can access your personal email account, games and the internet without viewing any work-related material.

>Choosing your hours

One significant benefit of homeworking is that you may no longer have to do a standard working day. Even if you do early or late shifts, or your hours vary on different days of the week, it is important that your time is structured, but for many people there is a lot to be gained from looking outside the nine-to-five.

Sometimes it is a matter of practicalities. You may have decided to homework as a way of fitting your career in around other commitments or altering your lifestyle for the sake of your health. That is obviously relatively straightforward if you have also gone part-time, but if you finish at 3pm to do the school run or take Wednesday afternoons off to attend a course and have to make those hours up elsewhere then mastering your routine can be more of a challenge.

Predictably, the first rule is that your substitute work time has to be set in stone. You can't tell yourself you'll just work late – or worse, through lunch – on a couple of other days to make up for it, and expect things to fall into place. Can you commit to working, say, Saturday mornings instead? And if so, can you arrange your tasks so that your work is not compromised by colleagues and clients being out of the office over the weekend?

It may, of course, be your job itself that sets the agenda – if you have to deal with a lot of people in other time zones, for example. That can work well if it suits you to have more personal or family time during the day and you are happy to sacrifice evenings out, but beware the endless social calls from friends who've just finished and are putting their feet up. And do ensure you schedule in some definite relaxation time for yourself. It may sound like an ideal set-up for parents with young children but it can really only be successful if you finish the leisure part of your day feeling refreshed and ready for work, not exhausted and longing for a bath or a glass of wine.

It is also worth giving some thought to what your own peak times are individually. Are you a bright morning person who's starting to flag by lunchtime or the quintessential night owl? It may not be realistic to base your hours entirely on when you are feeling most productive – unless, perhaps, you are a novelist or an artist who doesn't need to communicate or collaborate with anyone else to work – but employing a little flexibility to make the most of your natural clock can make a marked difference. Would it be a problem for colleagues or your business if you started very early when you are feeling most energised and took a longer lunch break with an early-afternoon siesta? Even if it's not possible to change your overall hours, experts recommend matching tasks to your varying energy levels throughout the day. For most people, that means tackling the most complex or creative elements of your job in the morning or late afternoon, and working through more mundane filing and emailing during the post-lunch slump.

>Stay focused

Just because you no longer have a manager calling spur-of-the-moment progress meetings or colleagues hovering beside your desk to share the latest gossip, it doesn't mean the distractions at home are any less compelling. If you are a domestic god or goddess, you may be unsettled by the knowledge that there's washing waiting to be hung up, breakfast dishes in the sink or meat that really ought to be in the slow cooker by mid-morning. For the less industrious, there's the lure of the television, the sofa or the corner shop (with nobody to ask where they're going). And it's many times harder to get into work mode if there's someone else in the house, whether it's your partner having a lie in, your flatmate chatting over coffee or the children playing in the hall.

The best way to deal with domestic chores is to actually incorporate them into your schedule. That obviously doesn't mean you can devote huge chunks of your working day to mowing the lawn or redecorating the dining room, but if you plan the short breaks you should be giving yourself anyway to coincide with the washing machine finishing its cycle or the last collection from the post box at the end of the road then you'll be giving your eyes a rest from the screen, getting your body moving again and dealing with those time-sensitive jobs while you are at it. Plus if you know you have allocated a slot for them to be sorted out, you won't be continually worrying about forgetting them. Just make sure you stick strictly to the time limits on those breaks.

If the distractions are making greater demands on your time and energy, you need to reassess exactly what your responsibilities and commitments are. Time management experts say they frequently see situations where the partner who is based at home is the one expected to sort out any domestic crisis from organising a plumber to collecting a sick child from school, regardless of whether their work is more important to the household income. Even if on some occasions there is a practical reason for this, such as the length of your partner's commute, you really have to sit down together and discuss alternative measures. It is also important that you make clear from the start to your children and anyone else who may be in the house precisely what your working hours and conditions are. Genuine emergencies aside, be specific about what you are and aren't prepared to be interrupted for.

Within your office, take an honest look at all the papers, magazines and e-newsletters you subscribe to and pick out those that are really necessary for work. The others either cancel or divert to a personal email address.

>Efficient communication

Maximising your productivity isn't just about removing outside distractions – most people unintentionally waste time on a daily basis just by approaching normal tasks in an ineffective manner. Change the way you use elemental tools such as the phone and email to streamline your working day.

Email

▶ Change your computer settings so that emails are only delivered into your inbox every 15 minutes, half an hour or hour depending on the nature of your job and how quickly they are likely to require a response. This isn't irresponsible – if someone needs to contact you with something urgent, they will pick up a phone – and it will stop you being continually distracted by things that will, in the main, turn out to be lower priorities than what you are working on.

▶ Use the signature facility on your email to write templates of short messages you are frequently retyping – acknowledgements, directions, fees information and so on. For longer sections of text, save them all on one Word document and keep it minimised on your screen so you can copy and paste them whenever needed.

▶ Before you start writing an email, question whether it's really the best form of communication for the task in hand. No one can type as fast as they talk, speedily thrown-together emails tend to be littered with typos and often unclear, and if the subject is ambiguous or contentious, written as opposed to spoken messages can be easily misconstrued.

▶ If you don't require a reply to an email, flag that fact up in the subject line or right at the top. It will save you, as well as the recipient, time by preventing your inbox being clogged up with acknowledgements and other unnecessary messages.

▶ Keep your email format simple. Use text rather than HTML and avoid using font styles and colours. You will only waste time to-ing and fro-ing if the recipient's machine isn't configured for them.

Phone technique

▶ If you go through to voicemail, include details of when you will be available to receive the return call on your message. If you need to make regular calls to someone, agree a time that should always be mutually convenient.

▶ Begin calls by apologising for only having a brief window for the conversation so the other person is aware of a time constraint from the start. Phoning just before natural cut-offs such as lunch and the end of the working day should mean you are both equally keen to stay prompt and to the point.

▶ Buy a wireless headset. Not only are they better for your posture, but they free up your hands to get on with mundane filing or other minor tasks while you are on the phone.

▶ Unless a call is going to be extremely brief and straightforward, make a note in advance of the points you want to make and the information you need to get. It will help keep the conversation focused and prevent you having to phone back later.

▶ Group your calls and make them one after another. Having a list to work through will naturally make you more efficient and less inclined to get sidetracked.

▶ Don't be tempted to ignore a ringing phone unless you are right up against a deadline. Answering it, even if turns out not to be relevant or important, will almost certainly be quicker than trying to trace the caller or listening to a message, noting contact details and phoning back.

▶ If all else fails, research shows that getting out of your chair and making calls on your feet typically reduces their length by a minute or two each.

>Leave home

No matter what precautions you take against other interruptions, your home office space will inherently be full of distractions in the form of essentials such as the phone, fax, internet and email. In the same way that most office workers occasionally take projects home where they instinctively feel they will be better able to concentrate on them, you may sometimes need a change of scene. It might sound contradictory to leave the environment you have carefully created to match your needs, but it can really help to clear your mind and give you some space to think if you can get away from all the trappings of the office temporarily. It doesn't matter where you go. Sometimes just retreating to another room in the house where you can't hear the beeping of the fax machine is enough. Otherwise decamp to your local library, coffee shop, park or National Trust property – anywhere that you can just take your notebook or laptop. Switch your phone onto silent or, better, leave it at home, and don't log in to your email.

>Do to-do lists help?

Loved and loathed in equal measure, the to-do list in one form or another is seen as an essential by almost every time management professional. But their recommended methods do vary significantly, and it's really a matter of personal experimentation to see what suits you – whether it's a colour-coded or computerised planner, or a never-ending piece of paper, complete with crossings-out and arrows, which at least gives you a constant reminder of what you have already achieved.

The biggest issue is how to prioritise what's on your list, and the most crucial thing to remember is that urgent and important are not the same thing. If you are constantly working to stay on top of immediate tasks, those with no short-term deadline but a greater pay-off in the long-term are in danger of being postponed indefinitely. Try adapting one of these methods from leading time management consultants to suit your working style:

▶ Step back from your list and appraise everything on it for how important, rather than how pressing, it really is – using a three-tier system for high, medium and low is usually enough. Then work out your priorities list accordingly, initially ranking items for urgency only within those marked as being of high importance, then medium. Tasks with a low importance rating should be delegated, delayed to a quieter or less productive time, or crossed off entirely.

▶ Rather than reacting instantaneously to everything that comes through (or putting it off for an unspecified later that may never arrive), make a decision and put the task down on your list either for today or tomorrow. That automatically means you are forced to think about it and puts in a buffer which allows you to order your work properly. Have a page-a-day task diary and unless something is really urgent, write it in under tomorrow's date. Those items don't then need to be prioritised because the important thing is that you make every effort to get through the lot – you are trying to clear them each day. A closed list is meant to be a very effective way of processing work, and you can also see very clearly when you have more on than you can handle. Larger projects will obviously have to be broken down into sub-tasks so that they're manageable within the system. If you are looking at a specific long-term commission, schedule in the final deadline and then work backwards, putting in completion dates for the various stages.

▶ Unless something is truly urgent or, during a very busy period, can obviously wait with no ill effects, group tasks according to the action they require you to take. Making phone calls several or all at a time, reading and returning emails once or twice daily rather than as they are received, holding meetings or teleconferences one after the other, and running errands one or two days per week rather than on a daily basis can all help to maximise efficiency and ensure everything on your list gets done without you having to allocate individual importance.

There are many other possible approaches and lots of authors and consultants on the subject offer a surprising amount of free advice on their websites (see 'Resources'), so if one system doesn't work for you and your work or other commitments, it is well worth trying another.

Whichever method, or combination of methods, you choose, there are obvious practical exceptions to your main prioritisation principles if you have to deal with a colleague or client who's in another time zone or only works mornings, for example. And most experts warn against over scheduling your day. Some even advise that you plan for just 50% of your time, leaving you with the flexibility to handle interruptions and unplanned emergencies. Schedule routine tasks for times when you expect to be interrupted, and save (or make) larger blocks of time for your priorities.

The bigger picture:

When you're cramming your to-do list with tasks, don't forget to write down periods of strategic thinking or forward planning. This is important whether you are running your own business – in which case it is vital to step back on a regular basis and monitor the direction in which its going and what changes need to be made – or working as an employee. Homeworkers as a whole feel they are less likely to be promoted than their office-based counterparts and while prejudice (and paranoia) may play a part in this, it may also be true that they contribute less beyond the parameters of their normal daily job. If you are missing out on strategy meetings that are taking place in the office – formally or informally over the desks – then you need to

devote time to getting up to speed with where the company is heading overall and looking at how you can develop your own role.

The same is true if you are still unhappy with your work – life balance and feel that elements of your current set-up are having a negative impact on the way you work or how you are included in the life of the company. Set time aside to think about solutions so you can present something positive rather than negative when you ask for changes to be made.

It is all too easy to get bogged down in everyday tasks, but looking ahead is crucial and not something to be relegated to odd spare minutes in the car or bath.

>Employ incentives

If you are struggling to find the motivation to tackle particularly large, difficult or uninspiring tasks on your list, or know that you are slipping into procrastination, there's nothing wrong with bribing yourself. There are top executives who keep bags of sweets in their desk drawers as little rewards for jobs completed! Promising yourself five minutes in the sun in the garden or lying in a darkened room with your eyes closed is obviously better for your waistline,

'If you add up the hours, I do a long working day but because it's spaced out it's very easy to manage'

and for giving you a boost before you return to your desk, but just make sure whatever you are treating yourself to is reasonable in proportion to the work required, doesn't take more than 10–15 minutes out of your working hours and doesn't interrupt the overall structure of your day. Never promise yourself, for example, that you'll have a lunch break just as soon as this project's done – it will be counter-productive.

>Start saying no

If you have put streamlined systems into action and cut back on all outside distractions, and your to-do list is still impossible to stay on top of, you simply have too much work. In some cases it is predictable; if you were buried under the size and weight of your responsibilities in the office, that isn't going to change simply because you have moved location. If you have started homeworking in order to launch your own business then you are probably in charge of every single aspect in a way you will never have been as an employee, however senior.

How you deal with an excessive workload will obviously depend on your role within the company. Employees really need to schedule a meeting with the boss to discuss reasons and possible solutions. It is important you do this sooner rather than later. Good managers will recognise when someone is struggling in the office, but if you are out of sight at home you can't expect them to read your mind.

If you are running your own business, it's very easy to let your job spiral out of control and experts recommend having a commitment pruning session at least every couple of months. Make a list of everything you do and ask yourself how important each one is to the business. At the end of the day, are some of them unnecessary? If the list is still too long, then the tasks on it must be valuable enough to the success of your company to spend money on them – so work out which ones you could most usefully outsource. Alternatively, of course, it may be time to look at taking on an extra employee. Similarly, if you are self-employed you will either have to accept fewer commissions or look at the impact on your work, lifestyle and finances of expanding into a two-person operation.

'I also use the phone far more... I was wasting a lot of time writing [emails] and waiting for replies'

If you already have people working under you, the general rule most professionals follow is that if one of your staff can do it 80% as well as you can, delegate it. Recalculating your true hourly rate on a regular basis – and comparing it to what you pay others – may help you let go.

It worked for me...

Alia, 48, North London

Alia has worked from home for six years. She says:

'My hours are unusual and wouldn't suit everyone but they fit in really well with my family commitments. I'm lucky that because I have to deal with colleagues in America for my job, and they don't usually get into the office until tea time here, I can take more of my leisure time during the day and do another stint of work in the evening after my son Max is in bed.

Our routine is pretty much set in stone – I've found it has to be or everything descends into chaos. I get up at 6am, arm myself with coffee and toast and shut myself away in my home office until 8.30am. I start so early because there are often urgent messages from overnight that people are waiting for responses to, plus I have my best ideas at that time – I'm a real morning person – and it means I can make use of the time while my husband is still in the house. He gets Max up and dressed and makes his breakfast, and then I take over when he leaves for work. I do the school run and then do any shopping and errands on the way home. I spend the rest of the morning sorting out all the domestic stuff – washing, cleaning and any preparation for dinner – then I have an early lunch and work from 12.15 until 3pm when I have to do the school pick-up. I have the rest of the afternoon to spend with my son, we all eat together as a family when my husband gets home, I get Max settled and then it's back into the office from 8.30pm until 11pm or sometimes midnight.

If you add up the hours, I do a long working day but because it's spaced out it's very easy to manage, and as I work at the quietest times in our house I get a lot done. I also get to spend plenty of quality time with my son, which is the main reason I wanted to work from home.'

It worked for me...

Emma, 25, Manchester

Emma, has worked from home for a year. She says:

'When I first started working from home it was like I reverted to being a student again. I was justifying getting up late almost every day because I was too tired to be productive, taking far too many coffee breaks, and spending all morning doing things I 'just needed to get out the way' so I could concentrate on work. Then I'd end up at the computer all night before deadlines. And I kept having to cancel things I'd arranged to do in the evening because I was so far behind.

Fortunately for me, it was actually part of our company policy to encourage homeworking and lots of people had started doing it at the same time as me. We had a few meetings to discuss how it was going and there must have been others having similar problems because the company arranged a one-day time management course for everybody. I can't say I've put all of it into practice – I'm not really a colour-coding kind of person – but I've been surprised at how much of a difference properly timetabling my day makes. If I know I have other things I need to do within working hours like sorting out household bills or just putting the washing on I actually allocate short breaks to do them – and make a cup of tea and stretch my legs at the same time. It's no different to people having cigarette breaks in the office. Then it's straight back to my desk because I know I've only got a couple of hours or whatever until lunch and I have things flagged up to be completed by then.

I also use the phone far more. I'd got into the habit of using email for everything but I now realise that I was wasting a lot of time writing them and waiting for replies, especially when the subject was complicated or up for debate and I was having 'conversations' that were going back and forth all day.'

Resources:

Useful websites

Time management and productivity tips

- ▶ Idea Mountain: www.ideamountain.com
- ▶ Mark Forster: www.markforster.net
- ▶ Steve Pavlina: www.stevepavlina.com
- ▶ Laura Stack: www.theproductivitypro.com
- ▶ Peter Turla: www.timeman.com
- ▶ Debbie Williams: www.organizedtimes.com

Further reading

- ▶ *Do It Tomorrow and Other Secrets of Time Management* by Mark Forster (Hodder & Stoughton)

The author's approach differs from that of most other time management professionals (no prioritising and a very cautious attitude towards to-do lists, for a start) so those who've previously struggled to find a system that works for them often become enthusiastic fans.

- ▶ *Eat that Frog!* by Brian Tracy (Hodder Mobius)

Not as eccentric as the title makes it sound, this is a no-nonsense guide to identifying those tasks that are truly important and eliminating the rest.

- ▶ *The Time of Your Life* by Tony Robbins (www.tonyrobbins.com)

A multi-media program including 16 CDs, a workbook and a personalised online time assessment tool among other things, it promises to provide you with all the tools you need to create your own effective system.

- ▶ *The Time Trap* by Alec Mackenzie (Amacom)

Widely considered to be *the* classic time management handbook, it is packed with practical advice but some of it will be of more use to managers with staff than, say, a self-employed homeworker.

Health and wellbeing

7

For many people, becoming a homeworker marks an opportunity to ditch the convenience food habit, eliminate the hours spent slouched behind the wheel or contorted in the corner of a crowded tube carriage, and play those long-promised games of tennis. The potential to make big, positive changes to your lifestyle is certainly there. After all, with no travel you should have extra leisure time, your working hours may be more flexible and you will no longer have to run the gauntlet of the vending machine several times a day. But it is disappointingly easy to replace one set of bad habits with another.

In a lot of cases, cutting out the commute means you no longer walk or cycle to the station. Stocking up on lunches at the supermarket instead of heading for the local café might improve your diet (and your bank balance) but it can also deprive you of that daily stroll in the fresh air. Combine that with the fact that you may be losing your corporate gym membership at the same time as you gain free access to the fridge, and far from kickstarting your new fitness regime, homeworking could see you piling on the pounds.

A sedentary lifestyle can have more immediate, serious consequences than a spreading waistline. Spending hours on end sitting at a desk puts pressure on your back and joints, and those stretches in front of a computer can also lead to eye strain and headaches. Back pain is already the most common health problem for workers in the UK and it is on the increase, rising by an alarming 5% between 2007 and 2008. There are numerous steps you can take and useful products you can buy as preventive measures, but the central issue is the amount of time the average homeworker spends sitting still. Those living alone or entrepreneurs working impossibly long hours to get a business off the ground are particularly at risk. In a warning to homeworkers everywhere, a Bristol-based computer programmer nearly died after spending 12 hours at a stretch in front of his home PC. He developed a pulmonary embolism when the blood clot in his leg travelled to his lungs.

Fortunately it's not all doom and gloom. Survey after survey shows that people who work from home take less time off sick. While this is partially explained by factors other than superior health – including lesser motivation among office workers and an understandable reluctance to travel or spread their germs among colleagues – university researchers who carried out studies in the UK noted not just statistics on sick leave but a significantly better work–life balance and improved wellbeing among homeworkers. In most cases, it's just a matter of making a few simple changes or additions to your regular routine to ensure that one of the principal benefits of homeworking isn't sacrificed to other pressures and commitments.

>Rise and shine

There is a temptation to wander straight from the bedroom into your office and start checking emails while the kettle boils, but making clear delineations between personal and work time and setting yourself up properly for the day will help you both physically and psychologically. Don't let yourself stay in bed until five to nine because you no longer have a train to catch. Unless you are really sleep deprived, early morning should naturally be the time at which your energy levels are highest, so make the most of it. Try setting an alarm, having a light snack as soon as you get up and then going for a run or to the gym, or even for a brisk walk with the dogs. If you have to do the school run, is it possible to leave the house earlier and either walk or cycle there?

Factor in time to get showered and eat a decent breakfast before you start work rather than balancing a plate of toast on your paperwork (studies show that eating a healthy breakfast every day can boost brainpower and aid decision-making as well as weight control. See 'Food for thought' below for suggestions). That way you will arrive at your desk ready to give work your full concentration. The endorphins released by your workout should keep you feeling upbeat and invigorated for several hours, your muscles will be warmed up so you are less likely to suffer stiffness or strains even if your posture isn't always perfect, and the slow-release carbohydrates will keep you going until lunchtime without an energy slump. Plus you can feel virtuous all day and won't be worrying about fitting in some exercise later.

>Time to get fit?

Lack of time is the most common excuse for failing to exercise and homeworkers could do with a few extra hours in the day as much as anyone. Frequently the commute is instantly replaced by other family and domestic commitments such as school runs and vital chores, and, if allowed, these would often cut short the working day and fill every scheduled break too. You need to take control of your daily routine to keep a fair and manageable balance between home and work – see Chapter 6 for practical tips on doing so – but you also need to reassess where exercise lies on your mental priority list. There is scientific evidence that exercise has huge benefits not only for your long-term health and wellbeing but also for your job, both directly and indirectly. It helps you to focus, boosts your energy and enthusiasm, reduces the number of sick days you take and promotes better sleep, which in turn also improves your concentration and productivity. It needs to be seen not as a luxury but as an essential, and given due prominence on your to-do list.

If you really can't fit in even a short exercise session before work, look at other times when you will gain the greatest possible advantage. Getting your heart pounding at lunchtime will help to stave off the common early afternoon slump, when people otherwise tend to work slowly and ineffectually, and find themselves easily distracted. Alternatively, use a pre-arranged game of tennis, football practice or session with a personal trainer to mark the end of the working day, ensuring you don't linger at the computer and that you have an immovable deadline to work towards. In addition to cementing the structure of your day, joining a class or a team can give you a new social network, something that is often lost when you leave the office environment with its shared lunches and after work drinks.

No one needs a full workout every day. Experts advise that if you are trying to increase your fitness or lose weight, you should aim for at least half an hour five times a week, while three times a week is normally sufficient to maintain your current levels. That applies to moderate activity (where you are breathing more deeply and your heart is beating faster but you can still carry on a conversation) not intense training. If you have a physical reason not to undertake most formal exercise, consider buying a pedometer.

You can also tailor your exercise choices to help you deal with the demands of your job and the way you react to them personally. If you need a physical outlet for stress and frustration try taking up something with a high tempo and the opportunity to use your strength and push yourself. Squash, tennis, running and classes like boxercise are popular choices. If you just want to let go of your stress and anxieties and create some inner calm, yoga and pilates have a spiritual element and will leave you with some stretches and relaxation techniques you can use at your desk. They also work on your posture, which can be crucial to avoid back and other musculoskeletal problems.

Definition:

Pedometer:

An electronic device that can be worn on a belt or waistband and calculates the number of steps taken by detecting hip movement. Some can also be calibrated to an individual's stride to measure distance covered. Pedometers experienced a surge in popularity in the mid-Noughties with people keen to discover just how sedentary their daily routine really was. They act as a reminder and a motivation to achieve the recommended 10,000 steps a day, even if that means pacing up and down your home office during phone calls.

>Are you sitting comfortably?

Depending on when you started your last office job and the Health & Safety culture within the company, you may dimly remember being shown how various levers could be operated on your desk chair. If you ever used or even thought about them again, you will undoubtedly have been in the minority. Despite growing awareness of the potential negative side effects of a desk job, as more and more people spend the greater part of their working lives in front of a computer screen, attitudes remain blasé. Do you generally work on the principle that if your legs fit under the table, your chair's the right height? Once you are ensconced at your desk do you stand up regularly to ease your back and joints, or are you not even conscious of how much time has gone by? Research by the British Chiropractic Association concluded that 32% of the population spends more than 10 hours a day sitting down, while for 16% it's more than 12 hours.

The general rule is never to remain seated in the same position for more than 40 minutes at a time. You should also take the opportunity to stretch and strengthen your spine on a regular basis. The British Chiropractic Association has put together an easy-to-follow three-minute posture care programme with 12 on-the-spot exercises that could be done in your home office at any time. Visit www.straightenupuk.org and download the free leaflet.

Probably the single most important thing you can do to protect your back, though, is to ensure you are using a properly adjusted ergonomic chair suitable for the level of use you require. There is almost twice as much pressure on your back when you are sitting incorrectly as there is when you are standing up. If you are unable to find a chair that works perfectly for you, there are accessories on the market that will help. Be aware of other postural habits that may be detrimental such as cradling the phone between your ear and shoulder, which puts undue strain on your neck and shoulder muscles, and take steps to address them too. Run through this checklist when you set up your workspace and again, briefly, every morning in case anything has changed, moved or been forgotten.

► Is the seat of your chair at the correct height?

Many people set it too high but your lower arms and hands should be horizontal when you are using the middle row on the keyboard, with your wrists straight and your upper arms hanging vertically. It can be hard to judge yourself so if possible ask someone to watch you from the side.

► Do you need a footrest?

If your feet don't sit comfortably flat on the floor, it could affect your posture and circulation so find a suitable box or piece of board or buy a footrest. Most will allow you to adjust the height and the angle, though it does not actually need to be tilted unless you wear heels or prefer to sit with it a long way under the desk.

► Is the space under your desk clear?

Don't use it for storage because you need sufficient room to stretch and move your legs and feet.

► Are your elbows directly below your shoulders when you are typing?

You should move your chair forwards or backwards until they are. If you are prevented from getting far enough forward by the armrests, you will need to either remove them or replace the chair.

▶ Do your lower arms get some support from the armrests when your upper arms hang down naturally?

Many non-adjustable armrests tend to be set too low, which will encourage you to slump in your chair. You can wrap foam or fabric around them to raise the height while giving padding, and you may well need to add more than 5cm for the position to be right.

▶ Does your chair rotate freely?

You should be able to reach everything you need at your desk without twisting your body or overstretching.

▶ Is the backrest giving good support?

When you sit upright, it should fit fully into the curve of your lower back. If it doesn't, or you have to use a straight-backed chair, consider buying a lumbar support cushion that can be moved and fastened to other chairs as required.

▶ Do you require a headset?

If you intend to use your hands for typing or taking notes during calls then it's an essential purchase. Depending on the nature of your work, it might be worth investing in a more expensive model with a greater range and longer talk time so you can stretch your legs, get some fresh air or even do basic domestic tasks during routine calls.

▶ Could software help?

There is now at least one program on the market that uses a webcam to continually check your posture in front of the computer. If you sit in a consistently bad posture for longer than a minute or two at a time, a reminder appears on screen.

>Safe computer use

Where the use of visual display units (VDUs) forms a significant part of your normal work as an employee, your employer has a legal right under Health & Safety regulations to provide or ensure the following, whether or not you work from home:

▶ You must have breaks or changes of activity, and ideally have some discretion over when to take them. Their length and regularity, however, is not specified.

▶ Eye tests by an optometrist or doctor must be provided and paid for if requested. But your employer only has to pay for your glasses if special ones are needed and your usual ones can't be used.

▶ You must be provided with training and information on how to avoid problems as a result of VDU use, and also on the steps that are being taken by your company to combat them.

Suitable advice leaflets employers can use for this purpose can be downloaded from www.hse.gov.uk. These also act as useful checklists that can be easily stuck on the wall for homeworkers who are self-employed or running a business and responsible for their own wellbeing when using computers. Omitting to take any steps to ensure your computer area is correctly set up and used can result in eye strain, headaches or migraines, RSI-style problems with your hands and wrists, and even pain in your back, neck and shoulders. Take the following into consideration and reassess your workspace and your own routines regularly.

Positioning

▶ The top of the computer screen should be at or just below eye level. If it is too low you will need some form of riser, whether it is a monitor arm, a height-adjustable platform or simply a suitable box or even book.

▶ To view the screen comfortably, it should be around 55–65cm away. Much further and you will be putting unnecessary strain on your eyes. If you feel you need it a lot closer, ask yourself why as there could be a problem with the quality or settings of the screen or with your eyesight.

▶ Place your monitor square on, directly in front of you. Don't be tempted to use the corner of an L-shaped desk for

> **Definition:**
>
> **RSI:**
> RSI (repetitive strain injury) is the damage that can be caused to nerves, tendons and other soft tissues by continuous use of the same limited movements over time, such as when regularly typing all day without sufficient breaks or support for your arms and wrists. Symptoms are normally pain and numbness, and muscles may become weaker.

your computer because you will almost inevitably end up twisting your back or neck.

▶ You should keep the mouse as close to you as possible – at least near enough to use it with your upper arm hanging down vertically and relaxed. If the mouse tends to creep away as you use it, try taping the mouse mat (or a cut-down version to save space) in place on the desk.

▶ Don't assume you need to use the feet on the keyboard to have it angled towards you. This is only necessary if your elbows are below desk height.

▶ Your monitor should be positioned to avoid glare from overhead lights and from sunlight for as much of the day as possible. Never site your desk with your back directly to the window unless there is an alternative source of natural light so you can draw the blinds or curtain when required.

Chair considerations:

○ Is the seat of your chair at the correct height?

○ Do you need a footrest?

○ Is the space under your desk clear?

○ Are your elbows directly below your shoulders when you are typing?

○ Do your lower arms get some support from the armrests when your upper arms hang down naturally?

○ Does your chair rotate freely?

○ Is the backrest giving good support?

○ Do you require a headset?

○ Could software help?

Products

▶ If you rest your wrists on the desk when you type, buy a gel wrist rest to support them, redistribute the pressure and help ensure you keep the correct hand position while using the keyboard. Some makes also have inbuilt antibacterial protection for a healthier work environment. Mouse-mats with integral gel wrist support can also help to prevent strain.

▶ Cut unavoidable glare and block most radiation, reducing the demands made on your eyes, with a filter for your screen if it's needed.

▶ Look for alternatives to using your laptop as your main computer because the screens are typically too small to be comfortable for your eyes over long periods, but if you have no choice at least make sure you have a docking station for it. This will allow you to adjust the height, preventing you causing injury to your neck, shoulder or back muscles by hunching over it.

▶ If you regularly refer to paperwork while typing, buy a document holder that you can position at the same height and distance from you as the monitor.

Good practice

▶ Get your eyes checked regularly and if you are prescribed glasses or contact lenses for computer use then wear them! They will often be a preventive measure to avoid straining your eyes further, so wearing them sporadically or not at all because you don't physically need them to read what's on the screen could lead to long-term damage.

▶ Give your eyes a brief break from the screen every 20 minutes, allowing them to refocus. This only needs to be for 20 seconds to have a positive effect. You should ideally have enough space behind your monitor to be able to look beyond it and relax your eyes. Each time you look away from the screen make a conscious effort to blink repeatedly. During VDU use, the rate at which you blink is significantly reduced, leading to dry, tired eyes. Aim to have a longer break every hour. You can rest your eyes completely by putting your palms over them and keeping them in total darkness for a minute. There are various forms of screen break software available that will flash a reminder message onto your screen at suitable intervals.

▶ Keep the screen clean, preferably by wiping it down at least three times a week, as a dirty screen increases the strain on your eyes. You can buy specialist preparations for this purpose, including environmentally friendly solutions, or use ordinary household supplies if you know exactly what you are dealing with. Monitors with glass screens can be cleaned with normal glass or window cleaner, sprayed onto a cloth and never directly onto the machine. If the screen has anti-glare protection or another special surface it could be damaged by glass cleaner and you should stick to water. An LCD screen should be wiped with a soft, dry cloth – paper towels could scratch it – or one dampened with surgical spirit if necessary.

>Exercise at your desk

Not even fitness gurus suggest you use your home office for a heart-pumping aerobic-style workout, though American scientists did recently create a combined workstation and treadmill so anyone with a spare £1,000 to spend could, theoretically, raise a sweat while finishing that report. More practically, what you can do even when sitting in front of your computer are a number of stretches tailored to the parts of your body most under pressure during long periods at your desk. Put together a short sequence and make it as integral a part of your day as switching on the PC. Stretching in the morning will help to loosen you up for the day, but running through a routine at night, too, can benefit your posture long term because your body then has the chance to get used to the mechanical changes in the muscles as you sleep. You can even just do three or four stretches each time you stop for a break throughout the working day.

Home office hygiene:

On average, the area where you put your hands on a desk harbours 10 million bacteria. You might expect that a home office, with just one occupant, would have a considerably lower eurgh-factor, but the chances are that as a homeworker you don't have professional cleaners dealing with your workspace, or certainly not on a daily basis as you may have done in a communal office. And studies suggest that regular cleaning does make all the difference in staying on top of a potentially health-threatening problem. In fact, bacteria levels can be reduced by 99.9%. Keyboards should be cleaned at least twice a week. There is a full range of cleaning fluids and accessories on the markets, including air dusters, which use compressed air to blast dust and debris away from inaccessible areas such as between the keys.

Don't push on through any pain or discomfort when stretching, increase the range of motion very gradually, and ensure you are warm when you start. Focus on the following areas when you are largely deskbound:

Neck

▶ Sit upright and, facing forward, try to touch your right shoulder with your right ear without moving, hunching or tensing your shoulders. Hold for a count of six. Repeat on the left side. Repeat six times. To deepen the stretch, drop the opposite arm and shoulder down as if reaching to the bottom of your pocket.

▶ Sit or stand with good posture and let your head drop towards your chest. Place one hand on the back of your head and one on your chin, then tuck your chin in and gently stretch the back of your neck by drawing your head towards your chest.

Eyes

▶ Roll your eyes around in a circle breathing out at they move downwards and in as they move upwards. If one direction is naturally easier, work more going the other way until they feel equal.

Shoulders

▶ Raise your shoulder and rotate two or three times forwards and then backwards, maintaining a good posture.

▶ Standing upright, straighten your arms and raise them out sideways, then turn your palms upwards. Without raising your shoulder, pull your arms backwards and gently squeeze your shoulder blades together.

Fingers

▶ With palms face down, simply spread your fingers as wide as you can and hold for a count of six. Then relax them.

Wrists

▶ Move your shoulders back and down, keeping your arms close to your body. Flex your wrist, make a fist, then rotate your wrist outwards.

Arms

▶ Straighten your arms out. Stretch your wrists back. Touch your shoulders and repeat.

▶ Bend your right arm above your head with your hand hanging down between your shoulder blades. Hold your right elbow with your left hand and pull it behind and towards your head. Feel the stretch and hold it for a count of six. Relax and repeat on the left.

Back

▶ Sit (or stand) with good posture. Place your hands on your lower back. Push your hips forward and your shoulders back to arch your spine. Relax.

▶ Stand with your feet apart and hands on hips. Gently twist, as far as is comfortable, to the right. Relax. Repeat on the left.

You can also incorporate squats, leg stretches and flexing your ankles, and core exercises. Ideally consult a personal trainer to work out the best routine for you, concentrating on any specific areas of weakness or concern.

Concentration techniques:

Whereas some people find it far easier to focus in the familiar surroundings and normally quieter environment of their own home, for others it is much harder to get into work mode and create the kind of tunnel vision that enables them to be productive. For practical tips of dealing with interruptions and household distractions, see Chapter 6. If the problem is to a greater extent internal rather than external, one or more of these techniques may work for you.

▶ Identify the natural rhythm of your day and go with it rather than trying to fight against it. That may mean you do your most intensive work first thing in the morning and schedule more mundane tasks that don't require high levels of concentration, such as filing and sending standard email replies, for those times when it is hardest to keep focused. Typically this is mid-to-late morning and for a longer period in the early afternoon, though everyone is different.

▶ Build in frequent changes. It is difficult to concentrate on any one thing for extended stretches of time, but if, when deadlines allow, you switch tasks every hour or so, you'll be using slightly different skills and calling on other parts of your brain, so it will be easier to keep up your powers of concentration without becoming tired.

▶ Don't try to do more than one thing at a time. Full concentration intrinsically means to the exclusion of all else, so it is impossible to focus properly on a job if you are attempting to tackle others simultaneously.

▶ Don't worry. Getting stressed about your workload, whether you are going to win that account or what you are planning to say to your boss just diverts attention away from the task in hand and, because it's emotion-based, tends to drain you of energy too. People who schedule in some 'worry time', when they can give free rein to all their concerns, report finding it easier to dismiss these thoughts the rest of the time.

▶ Take control of your thoughts. People commonly cast themselves as the hopeless victim of their own minds, but you can train yourself to block distracting ideas and prevent your mind wandering if you are determined enough. If your thoughts stray, clearly tell them to stop and get straight back to the job in hand. It is allowing yourself to become mentally sidetracked that inspires more irrelevant thoughts and takes you off into a time-wasting reverie.

▶ Try yoga or a meditation class, which will give you relaxation and visualisation techniques to improve your powers of concentration. Particularly if you are somewhat sceptical, these can have little effect at first but with practice you will feel more in control.

▶ As a starting point, set aside a few minutes in your working day just to be quiet. Make use of the fact that you are at home by using a bed or comfortable chair in a darkened room if it helps. Close your eyes and breathe deeply and regularly. Inhale through your nose slowly and deeply, being aware of your lower chest and stomach inflating. Hold for five seconds before exhaling deeply. Again, hold for five seconds. Try to focus entirely on your breath as it flows in and out of your body. If your attention wanders, gently pull it back to the feeling of your chest rising and falling. Do this for five minutes before letting your breathing return to normal.

>Food for thought

When you start working from home, you have a completely clean slate when it comes to overhauling your diet. With the ingredients and facilities on hand to make lunch rather than eating out, what's on the menu is entirely up to you, but if you want your food to play a part in helping you to work productively and maintaining your energy levels, there are a few basic principles to bear in mind.

Breakfast

Don't forget that breakfast literally means the meal that breaks the fast of the night before. If you are tempted to skip it, ask yourself whether you can reasonably expect your brain or body to function at anything close to optimum levels when they haven't been refuelled for 12 hours or more. You really will be running on empty, which will mean you either spend the morning feeling tired and sluggish and working ineffectively or you give in to cravings at around 11am and eat half a packet of biscuits – or both.

A proper breakfast doesn't have to be time-consuming. Your aim should be to stock up on complex carbohydrates that will release energy slowly and help to maintain your blood sugar levels, avoiding the slumps you get after very sweet or highly processed foods. Bread (ideally wholemeal), non-sugary breakfast cereals and porridge all fit the bill. When you have time, treat yourself to a healthy cooked breakfast of egg (not fried!) and grilled bacon, sausages and tomatoes. It will provide a psychological boost as well as all the energy and nutrients you need.

A glass of pure fruit juice or smoothie will give you a vitamin injection, be more refreshing and hydrating that coffee or tea, and count towards your recommended five-a-day of fruit and vegetables.

Lunch

It is important to have a proper break at lunchtime and sitting down (somewhere other than your desk) to eat a good meal will have psychological as well as physical benefits. Don't overstretch yourself though. Unless your routine is very unusual you won't want to take more than an hour away from your work at this time of day and the chances are that you will have domestic chores or 30 minutes of exercise to fit in too. Realistically, you are not going to be marinating peppers or whipping up a goat's cheese tartlet, so make sure when you stock up at the supermarket that you have plenty of quick, easy options available to you. And don't overlook last night's leftovers. If you have taken the trouble to cook something healthy for your evening meal, one of the advantages of being at home the next day is that any excess won't go to waste.

To avoid the infamous post-lunch slump, you again want to base your meal on starchy foods that will release energy slowly throughout the afternoon. A basic salad alone is unlikely to sustain you for long. Staples such as sandwiches, jacket potatoes, pasta, rice or couscous are all ideal if you choose the right filling, sauce or accompaniment. Go for any of the standard healthy-eating favourites – grilled chicken without the skin, prawns, cottage cheese, tuna, boiled egg – and opt for tomato-based soups and sauces, not the creamy or cheese-laden ones. Anything too rich will have you falling asleep at your desk as your body works to digest it. Add at least two portions of fruit and vegetables, and you should feel sufficiently energised to face the afternoon's workload.

Snacks

Unsurprisingly, dieticians recommend more fruit and vegetables for those peckish moments between meals. Chop up some raw carrot and celery into sticks at breakfast or lunchtime so you can just carry out a grab-and-go raid on the fridge and don't get distracted further. If you feel the need for something more substantial, toasted teacakes or slices of malt loaf are simple, healthy options that also help to maintain your blood sugars

Breaking bad habits:

If you find yourself mourning the loss of the vending machine or the coffee-and-cake stall at the station, try to identify what it is that you crave and keep a stash of healthier alternatives. Obviously the safest way to ensure you steer clear of biscuits, crisps and chocolate is just not to have any in the house, but if there are other people sharing your home that may not be a viable option. Particularly if you are trying to lose weight, don't fall into the trap of buying no snacks at all – you will almost certainly get so desperate that you go on a chocolate run to the nearest shop or tuck into something more substantial, such as a mound of buttered toast because it's all there is. Instead, have unsalted nuts or seeds on hand if you fancy crisps, dried apricots or mango if you are after something sweet, rice cakes to replace biscuits and perhaps a low-fat hot chocolate drink or small bar of dark chocolate for when nothing else will do.

What to drink

It can be tempting to keep the kettle constantly on the go, but you should ideally restrict yourself to no more than three cups of tea or coffee a day. Caffeine is proven to help concentration and boost wakefulness, but if you drink excessive quantities you will start to experience less pleasant side effects such as headaches, nausea and even shaking. Keep a bottle or jug of water on your desk and replace it from the fridge as you drink it or it goes warm. Though experts are still divided on the necessity to drink eight glasses a day, keeping well hydrated will help you combat headaches and some of the other potential problems derived from spending long stretches in front of a computer.

With up to 75% of employers across the country now banning the consumption of any alcohol during the working day, you are unlikely to be missing out on much drinking by working from home. By the same token, there's nobody to stop you opening a bottle of wine at lunchtime, but as even a small glass will exaggerate the natural dip in energy and alertness that almost everybody experiences in the afternoon, it's unlikely to be conducive to a productive work session. Save it for a sundowner and give yourself something to work towards!

It worked for me...

Simon, 55, East Sussex

Simon has worked from home for two years. He says:

'The chance to do more exercise was probably the main reason I chose to work from home. I'd lost quite a lot of weight by running, playing squash and tennis and watching what I ate following a bit of a health scare, but I was finding that spending all day sitting in my car and at my desk, it was all piling back on. The office was too far away to walk or cycle and the culture was very much that everyone went out for lunch together, normally to the local pub. I tended to work late anyway, so by the time I got home I just wanted to eat dinner and relax. You can get away with living like that for a while but I am getting older and I was concerned that if I continued that way I would be a heart attack waiting to happen.

Now I go running in the early mornings because I don't have to be fighting my way through traffic to work, and I play squash locally a couple of lunchtimes a week. Which means I can spend the evening in a restaurant or on the settee without feeling too guilty. I also eat much more healthily during the day. I still go out for lunch sometimes because I like to have a proper break from work, but not to the pub, and I don't think I've had chips at lunchtime since I started working from home.

I bought a gel wrist pad to use with my keyboard after I injured my wrist playing squash and became a bit more aware of supporting it. That took a short while to get used to but it is definitely a more comfortable position for typing. I've got a friend who's a trained physio to adjust the various

continued

movable parts on my chair because I apparently had it all wrong, and she also said my computer screen was too low for me so I got a platform for that. I do sometimes get headaches while I'm working but then I drink too much coffee and I'm not very good at taking screenbreaks – once I'm involved in something I lose track of time unless I have an appointment or I realise I'm hungry – so that's my own fault.'

Resources:

Useful websites

▶ Active Places: www.activeplaces.com

▶ BBC Health: www.bbc.co.uk/health

▶ British Nutrition Foundation: www.nutrition.org.uk

▶ Food Standards Agency: www.eatwell.gov.uk

▶ Healthy Living Scotland: www.healthyliving.gov.uk

Further reading

▶ *The BackSmart Fitness Plan* by Adam Weiss (McGraw-Hill Contemporary)

Exercises and principles for preventing and tackling back pain, recommended by many professionals in the field.

▶ *Nutrition for Dummies* (John Wiley & Sons)

Factual, unbiased look at just about everything you could need to know about the effects of your diet.

▶ *Office Yoga: 75 Simple Stretches for Busy People* by Darrin Zeer (Chronicle Books)

Easy-to-follow exercises organised by time of day and activity so you can find something to invigorate or calm you, or a stretch to do while you are reading emails or on the phone.

Sharing the space

8

There are many advantages to not living alone when you are a homeworker. Some people enjoy solitude but the lack of company can mean that you let your job take over and you often end up eating a ready-meal-for-one in front of your computer. There's no doubt that it's easier to stick to the planned structure of your working day when you know your flatmate or partner is going to walk through the door at 6pm and instantly switch the place into home rather than office mode. There is also the financial plus-point of having someone to share at least some of the overheads. And, of course, the opportunity to spend more time with your family may have been your overriding motivation for becoming a homeworker.

However, when there are other people involved, getting a harmonious balance between home and work can be particularly challenging. Hearing a key in the front door in the early evening may be a useful reminder that you are now into overtime, but if it's opening and closing repeatedly throughout the day, it can be an unwelcome distraction. A noisy game of football outside your office window could be annoying, but you wouldn't want children just to sit in front of the television or a video game. Similarly, it can be hard if your workspace is in the living room and your flatmate has invited friends round for dinner on the same night that you have a pressing deadline.

The last thing you want in a home – particularly one you don't get to walk away from in the morning – is an atmosphere of resentment. Unless you have a large property with your own self-contained (and soundproofed) office, issues will inevitably arise at one time or another. The answer is to anticipate them, discuss possible causes of contention with all members of the household and lay down ground rules and contingency plans for everybody to work with. A certain amount of compromise and understanding will be needed on all sides for your homeworking arrangements to be a success, but there are also practical steps you can take in advance to help keep everyone happy.

>If you have housemates

You probably wouldn't expect even your closest family to make major sacrifices for the sake of your homeworking career, and you can ask a great deal less of fellow tenants or lodgers. Your partner and children are likely to have a vested interest in the success of your work, both financially and emotionally, whereas housemates, even if they are friends, are paying for something. The power balance is obviously different depending on whether you are the landlord or you are both tenants, but regardless, the issue here is all about fairness.

As a matter of courtesy, you should discuss the implications of your decision to work from home before you actually make it. If anyone seems unhappy with the idea of an office in your shared living space, you should look carefully at whether you could be based in your own bedroom instead. There may still be some inconvenience in the form of extra phone calls and deliveries, but this set-up would otherwise have little impact on your housemates. If that isn't viable, perhaps you should use a small, wheeled computer desk that would be easily moved into your bedroom once other people return home or have a laptop fully loaded with everything you need to work so you can shut down your main office for the night and retreat out of people's way.

Be aware of whether or not the division of costs and labour around the home is fair. Utility bills will be affected by the energy consumption caused by your office and the use of lights, heating and kitchen appliances during the day when you are the only person there. You will also need to make similar calculations if you all pay into a communal kitty for food or a cleaner. Don't feel you have to wash up everybody's breakfast dishes, but you do have to be sensitive to potential niggles – are you creating more mess because you are taking coffee breaks and eating lunch at home, and, if so, are you doing proportionately more of the chores?

If the inconvenience to other housemates justifies it, you could offer to pay more rent or give them an appropriate discount if you are the landlord. There are other goodwill gestures that may also help, particularly in the overlap window as other people start to return home and you are still wrapping up work for the day. Installing a second television or some comfy chairs in the kitchen, for example, might create an alternative living space that would reduce the pressure. Or you could offset some of the disruption and rise in household costs by paying for the broadband or Wi-Fi connection that everyone else can then use.

Even if your arrangements are largely harmonious, inviting clients, colleagues or other business-related visitors into your shared home is a potential problem. Effectively these are strangers coming into contact with your housemates' personal belongings, either when they are not there or possibly when they are and are trying to get on with daily life. As most people have some concerns about holding business meetings on home turf anyway, it is almost certainly best for all concerned if you find an alternative venue away from the house. Look for premises with meeting and entertainment facilities, which you can use as often as you like for an annual fee. The right place will enhance your professional image as well as keeping your housemates on your side.

>If you live with your partner

When problems arise in this situation, it is often because one or both of you have unrealistic expectations. Homeworking can sound like the perfect arrangement if your partner is also in the house during the day, whether working or not. But if you or they are imagining that it will mean plenty more quality time together, there could be disappointments. Cutting out the commute should mean you have longer to share a pot of coffee in the morning, but enjoying lunches together may not happen as you try to keep your business head on or prefer for a midday workout in the gym like you always did at the office. Equally, if your partner isn't working and is continually trying to persuade you to have a lie-in, nip out for a coffee or help with a DIY job or the children, either your job or your relationship is likely to suffer.

Domestic chores can be a source of contention. All too often, it is simply assumed that whoever is at home will put on the washing machine, load the dishwasher and start dinner. It may well make sense for you to take on some household tasks, and it is possible to schedule them into your working day in such a way that they won't have a negative impact. However, if you are being asked to do things that call for more major changes to your routine you will need to discuss alternative plans. See Chapter 6 for ways to successfully juggle your job and other commitments at home.

If you both intend to work from home, look at your proposed office set-up and what it will mean in reality. A large number of couples who start out sharing workspace make other arrangements within the first few weeks. It may take up less room and keep more of your home free of work-related paraphernalia, but do you want to listen to all your partner's business calls and be overheard in all of yours? If the nature of your jobs means that one or both of you spends a large part of your working day on the phone, sharing in close proximity may not be a good idea. Also think of how your personal work styles compare. You may like to pace the room and listen to music to help the creative process but your partner might only be able to concentrate in peace and quiet. Even if your jobs are compatible, you need to look at whether your schedules and requirements will allow you to share technology such as an MFD and even a phone line or whether you will have to invest in a second printer, for example.

While it is essential with any home office to take steps to keep it separate from your living areas, it is particularly vital not to encroach on your personal space as a couple. You both need to be able to escape from your work so avoid setting up your workspace in your bedroom, however many other benefits it may have as a location.

>If it's a family home

If you are a homeworker, the chances that you are also a parent are getting higher and higher. Mothers in particular are increasingly seizing on home working as the happy medium between spending time with their children and continuing to fulfil their career potential. Whether they're negotiating flexitime after their maternity leave, buying into a family-friendly franchise, going freelance so they can choose the hours and contracts to suit them or launching their own business as a 'mumpreneur', working mothers are the fastest growing sector in homeworking. And the steps being taken by the government to extend the rights of parents and carers to flexible working patterns mean the numbers are only going to rise.

Some high-profile examples of women juggling business calls and Playdoh have also helped to boost awareness of homeworking as a viable option. The venture capitalists on *Dragons' Den* are approached week after week with ideas inspired by women's own experiences of parenting. Victoria Beckham recently came out as an unexpected proponent of homeworking, enthusing that her move to the USA had allowed her to run the family business empire from her own house with her three sons around her: *'I'm not the kind of mum who wants to palm my kids off all the time so it's a huge bonus for me that I can spend so much time with them now.'*

Not, as any 'normal' working parent would point out, that it's quite that simple. It's hard especially for young children to understand that Mummy or Daddy is in the house but not available to get them a drink or help them with their painting. How can you be at work when you are standing in the kitchen waiting for the kettle to boil?

The most effective solution is to make your office physically separate from the communal living space in your home. If you can work from a purpose-built shed in the garden or a loft conversion so you have your own floor, that's easy. It can still be done, though, even if your workspace is right in the heart of the house. Particularly if you have pre-schoolers, lock the door and pull down the blinds on any internal windows for the first few days until they have got used to the new arrangements – an out of sight, out of mind policy with children that age can be very successful. You might even want to consider buying a kettle and mini-fridge for your office so you don't get embroiled in family activities in the kitchen every time you want a cup of tea. If your desk is situated in the living room or other shared space, use a screen, décor and other design techniques to make it distinct from the rest of the room. This will help to draw a line psychologically between work and home, both for you and everyone else in the household. See Chapter 4 for practical suggestions on how to achieve this.

The boundaries will inevitably be blurred if your PC is used for homework, games and emailing in the evenings. This could mean that important files are accidentally moved or deleted (not to mention spillages and other accidents) and also has security implications. Do you vet all your children's friends? Can you be sure the emails they're opening are free of viruses? In one survey, 65% of teleworkers admitted they didn't know exactly who had had access to their home PC. If budget and space allow, it would be best to buy a basic machine for leisure use.

As well as delineating your physical workspace, you should also make it clear to everyone in the family – including any non-family members involved with childcare – what your working hours are and what constitutes an emergency for which you should be interrupted. Do bear in mind that if you are an employee and there is a crisis situation such as a sick child, you have the right to time off for dependants or emergency family leave. There is no maximum legal limit to this though one or two days are generally acceptable. Whether or not that time is paid, however, is down to your employer's discretion. You also have the right to request unpaid parental leave if, for example, your childminder is going on holiday and you are unable to make alternative arrangements. You are entitled to this if you have a child under five or a disabled child under 18 but you must give your employer three weeks' notice. In most cases, you can take a period of between one and four weeks off.

>Restructuring your working week

Trying to combine your job with family life by working from home can often leave you feeling tired, overloaded and somewhat out of control, The most likely reason is simply that you have taken on too much. Working full-time and being a stay-at-home parent are two potentially all-consuming jobs that can't be done simultaneously. Allowing your working hours to overrun into your leisure time in the evening to compensate for lost time and reduced productivity earlier in the day is not a solution. It may sound dramatic but it is important to address the issue before it threatens your health or your career.

Even if your initial motivation for working from home was to increase the amount of time you got to spend with your children, you may have to opt for part-time childcare as part of the answer. But you also need to look for a compromise in your work schedule. Employees who are not in a position to outsource or delegate any of their workload should approach their manager with an alternative flexible working proposal. Could you viably do compressed working, where you work for longer hours over fewer days? Or the opposite? Or you and your partner might have to calculate what it would mean to the family finances for you to work part-time or job share.

>Time for a career change?

Of course, it may be that your current career isn't suited to homeworking or other flexitime initiatives. It may be necessary for you to take an honest look at what is most important to you at this stage in your life. Would you be willing to sacrifice some portion of your salary and status at work in order to have more stress-free time with the kids? There is no job that is easy to combine with bringing up children, but some are definitely more family-friendly than others. If you are tempted to go down this avenue, though, do tread carefully. A number of supposed homeworking opportunities, generally advertised on the internet, have been exposed as scams with the remote offices impossible to track down and no payment forthcoming. If appropriate, try www.workingmums.co.uk, which has a database of more than 1,200 parent-friendly employers across the UK, or visit www.remoteemployment. com, where you can search extensive home based jobs listings. Alternatively, www. jobshare-uk.com showcases flexible working vacancies, www.mumandworking. co.uk specialises in part-time jobs for full-time mums or www.mumsclub.co.uk offers a guide to franchise opportunities suitable for homeworkers with children.

A family affair:

You might be surprised to discover that your children would like nothing more than to be involved with your work, especially if they can feel useful. The scope is probably very small if you are an employee, but numerous small home-based businesses have used a cheerful production line of family members to get products labelled, packaged and addressed for distribution.

If the products or services offered by the company are child related then kids tend to get an even bigger role, becoming inspiration and chief testers too. It's a great way to help children feel part of something, increase their understanding of what you do when you are 'at work' and of the basic principles of making and spending money and helping customers. I can also keep them occupied at times – plus their input could actually give added value to your business. Look at the way images of babies and children are used to market anything that manufacturers want to be perceived as gentle, natural or wholesome. If your children's involvement is genuine, putting family snapshots on your website and even asking them to help design your company logo or name new products in the range can all back up your credentials as a true family business. With the current backlash against the big chains and corporations in some areas, a reputation for a personal service can only be a good thing.

>Dealing with school holidays

A routine that works successfully for most of the year can be thrown into chaos by school holidays. Half-terms, Easter, even that never-ending summer break — they all have a nasty habit of creeping up on the unsuspecting homeworking parent. Of course, it can be a problem for office-based workers too, but because they usually already have childcare in place to cope with the school runs and after-school hours, they tend to be better prepared. With holidays you realistically have three main options. Which will work for your family depends on the flexibility your job, business or employer allows, your partner's situation, the budget you have available and your personal feelings about what constitutes a successful work–life balance. You can pay for childcare, you can change your routine or you can get help with work to free you up to look after the kids yourself. There are other options, such as essentially taking your children to work, but they are only really viable for a small minority of parents.

>Childcare

The most obvious solution is often to get the children out of the house – at least for the hours they would normally be at school. Trading days on parenting duty with other families can work if you are able to take time off when it's your turn to reciprocate, but if not – and you don't have doting grandparents on your doorstep – some form of organised (and paid for) childcare is frequently a necessity. All the possible choices carry their own advantages and disadvantages for homeworkers. As a working parent you may be entitled to some financial help with childcare so investigate your eligibility in advance – call the Working Families helpline on 0800 013 0313 or visit www.workingfamilies.org.uk – because if you are then your options will be restricted to early education childcare from a government-registered provider.

Nannies and home child-carers

Nannies and home child-carers are the most comprehensive, personal – and expensive – childcare available. Nannies can cost from £250 to £500 a week, depending on their hours and whether they live in. A home child-carer (a registered childminder working in your private house) will cost from around £130 to £300 a week. If you choose to employ a nanny, you need to remember that you will also be liable for National Insurance contributions, holiday and sick pay. You may also want to provide your carer with a mobile phone and possibly add them to your car insurance.

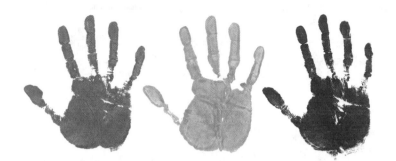

Nurseries and childminders

At a nursery or childminder's, your children are cared for alongside other people's in strictly controlled numbers, so you won't have input into how they spend their day in the way you would at home. Hours are also likely to be less flexible, though they are typically designed to cover a full working day and commuting time for parents who require that, so should allow plenty of leeway for homeworkers. Average costs are in the vicinity of £150 per week.

Crèches and playgroups

These tend to shut during the school holidays and also lack the longer hours and flexibility most full-time workers rely on.

Babysitters

Think about taking advantage of working from home by employing a babysitter. As they are unqualified (teenage schoolgirls frequently advertise their services locally), they may not be a suitable choice if you are leaving them alone with your children all day, but if they know they can knock on your office door in an emergency, they can be a good, cost-effective alternative. Expect to pay a minimum of £3.50 an hour.

Holiday clubs

These are the cheapest option of all, and also ensure your children are doing something other than watching television during their holidays – whether it's drama, archery or just chilling out with friends. Get details of your nearest Children's Information Service (CIS), which will provide information on holiday clubs in your area, from the parents' section at www.direct.gov.uk or ChildcareLink on 0800 096 0296. The hours are much longer than a school day (8am-6pm is common) and the average cost is under £100 a week.

>A new timetable

If full-time childcare isn't an option practically or financially – or it simply negates everything you were hoping to achieve in terms of work–life balance by becoming a homeworker in the first place – you will have to look at ways you can adjust your own workload to cater for your children. Self-employed homeworkers clearly have greater freedom to do this. If your business is contractual in nature, you could simply take on less work over holiday periods, though it is vital to factor this in from the start when calculating your finances for the year. You could then fit what you have left around part-time childcare or, depending on the ages of your children and their ability to entertain themselves for short periods, get by without having to pay for help at all. Downgrading your work commitments in this way, though, obviously does have a significant impact on your income and from a purely financial standpoint may not be worth it. For many people it will simply not be affordable.

> 'The nursery is ... cheaper than a private nanny so I have time and money to have fun with the girls after I pick them up'

Anecdotal evidence suggests that a considerable proportion of homeworking parents do just muddle through the school holidays. Spending the day at the park refereeing your children's football matches or pushing them on the swings, then turning on your computer when they've gone to bed, is far from ideal. Unless you are naturally a night owl, you are unlikely to be at your most productive, and you are liable to end up playing some very protracted games of phone tag. However, as a short-term measure that allows you some concentrated periods of work and some quality family time, it is undoubtedly the fallback position for many a working parent. If it looks like this will be your only option, giving your temporary arrangement some formal structure will help. Work out a timetable with the rest of your family so it's clear to everyone that you work Monday mornings and evenings, Tuesday afternoons and evenings, and so forth. The children can then schedule trips for the times you are off and know they need to have quieter time in the house when you are working if no alternative can be found.

Obviously it is also sensible to take most of your annual leave during school holidays, even if it means paying peak prices for everything, and at most companies it is worth getting this booked well in advance because you may be competing with other colleagues who have children. You could also discuss with your employer the possibility of working annualised hours, whereby your hours are worked out over the entire year rather than on a weekly basis. Most jobs require some level of consistency, but you may be able to do longer hours during term-time and work a four-day week over the holidays, for example.

>A helping hand

If you are an employee there is obviously little more you can do to ease your workload during holiday periods, but for those who are self-employed or running a small business, it may make financial sense to take on a part-time employee rather than paying out for childcare. This is particularly true if admin and other routine tasks take up a large portion of your time. Think about this as far in advance as possibly and work out exactly what help you will need and can afford. University students and older schoolchildren look for work specifically over the holidays, and if you are lucky you could arrange to have the same person coming back every year. The current levels of minimum wage are £3.40 an hour for under-18s who are no longer of compulsory school age, £4.60 for workers aged 18 to 21, and £5.52 for those who are 22 and above. If your business has never employed anyone before, you will need to ensure that your premises meet Health & Safety standards (see Chapter 11 for details) and also check the legal situation regarding your new employee's entitlements, paying tax and your other responsibilities. See www.hmrc.gov.uk/employers for more information.

> 'I do the same ... hours altogether that I always have ... but I really feel that I get a lot more time to be a mum.'

It worked for me...

Majanne, 40, nr Salisbury

Marjanne has been working from home for 18 months. She says:

'We employed a nanny when I started working from home because I liked the idea of being under the same roof as my two daughters, who were then aged three and one. She only worked four days a week because I have Mondays off for more family time but, through no fault of hers, the arrangement wasn't really right for us.

Every time I heard raised voices or one of the children crying, I'd stop what I was doing and have to fight the urge to go out and find out what was happening. And I think the girls found it quite confusing because they knew I was there and it was like I was deliberately ignoring them.

After a few months we made the decision to move them to a local nursery and they settled much better there. I wish we'd done it from the beginning. I get much more done because I am completely undisturbed in the house and I also get to work much earlier. When we had the nanny, I'd frequently wait for her to arrive so the children were occupied and I could go and get showered and dressed in peace, but now we have set times to drop the girls off I have to be ready and the moment I get back to the house at 8.40am I go straight to my desk. The nursery is also a lot cheaper than a private nanny so I have time and money to have fun with the girls after I pick them up at 3.30pm. I could leave them at the nursery later but that would defeat the object of working from home, so from then until bedtime at 7pm is our time. Then I'll catch up with any loose ends of work before my husband gets home at around 8.30pm.'

It worked for me...

Fiona, 34, Croydon

Fiona has been working from home for a year. She says:

'I requested to work from home part-time because I felt that, leaving early in the morning to get the train and not getting home until Ben's bath time, I was missing out on too much of my son growing up. The first arrangement I agreed with my manager was that I'd do three days in the office and two from home, but those days I didn't have to commute made me realise what a big chunk of time I was wasting just travelling when I could be eating breakfast with Ben and walking him to school, and still be back at the computer in my home office just a couple of minutes after 9am. I asked for another meeting and managed to persuade my company to let me do two extended days in the office and two and a half from home with Friday afternoons off to devote to special activities with Ben. Officially I finish at 1pm on Fridays but I tend to keep working until I need to leave on the school run. On other days Ben is collected by a childminder and he stays with her until 5.30pm. His dad picks him up on the days I'm at the office.

'I'm really happy with the set-up we have and grateful my company is so open minded about flexible working. I do the same number of hours altogether that I always have so my salary is unchanged but I really feel that I get a lot more time to be a mum. The only sacrifice I have to make in return is losing part of my evening on the days I work longer hours, but I try to get a very early train and make up at least some of the time at the beginning of the day because I find I get less tired if I do it that way round.'

Resources:

Useful websites

▶ British Franchise Association: www.whichfranchise.com

▶ Working Families: www.workingfamilies.org.uk

Childcare information

▶ ChildcareLink: www.childcarelink.gov.uk

▶ Daycare Trust: www.daycaretrust.org.uk

▶ National Childminding Association: www.ncma.org.uk

▶ National Day Nurseries Association: www.ndna.org.uk

▶ Ofsted: www.ofsted.gov.uk

Further reading

▶ *Working Mothers: The Essential Guide* by Denise Tyler (Need2know)

Full of no-nonsense advice, not just on the practical need-to-knows such as legal rights but the emotional issues too.

▶ *How to Succeed as a Working Parent* by Steve Chalke (Hodder & Stoughton)

A guide to achieving a good balance between work and family life, including factual advice on finding the right childcare and controlling your finances, and tips from those who've been there and done it.

Rural working

9

Hand in hand with the search for the perfect work–life balance in recent years has been the dream of escaping to the country. It is an aspiration that is fuelled on a daily basis by celebrities with home-grown vegetables and pigs in the garden, and property programmes packed with happy families trading in their suburban semis for Agas and orchards. And the consequences are tangible – and increasingly positive. The stories about irate locals burning down weekenders' cottages are being replaced by tales of regeneration, employment and support for rural businesses. As the traditional industries of the countryside continue to decline, advances in technology mean computer-based enterprises have moved in.

While small-scale business estates and live-work developments have blossomed in some rural areas, homeworkers are integral to the major shift that has been taking place. Recent statistics reveal that 11.6% of the rural workforce works from home, compared with 8% in urban areas, and the gap appears to be widening. Nationwide 39% of small businesses are home-based, but in rural areas it is 56%. That obviously includes some agricultural, equestrian and other traditional country businesses, particularly in areas such as the south west, but there are several indicators that it is the influx of former office workers that is making the difference. Around 100,000 people move from urban to rural districts of England every year and, with half of all home-based businesses in the countryside started up by incomers, they are paving the way for more to follow.

When the advance of broadband stalled in the early years of the 21st century, with coverage of around two-thirds of the UK complete but companies reluctant to invest in more remote areas, the rural communities themselves fought for better internet access. With large areas of the countryside considered too sparsely populated to make an upgrade worthwhile, BT – which despite a competitive broadband marketplace is currently virtually the only wholesale provider in rural areas – began putting figures on how many potential customers would have to register their interest in its high-speed ADSL service before it would act. Frustrated by the limitations of dial-up, local businesses and homeworkers led the campaigns, distributing leaflets, setting up websites and holding meetings to persuade others to sign up. In large part as a direct result of this, more than 99% of homes and businesses in the UK can now get broadband.

The cause was helped by the launch of numerous regional initiatives as part of the government's *Connecting the UK* strategy, providing subsidies and other financial support in an attempt to close the digital divide between urban and rural areas. With the 'true' countryside, as opposed to leafy commuter belts, drawing headlines as deprived and forgotten, the government has welcomed and actively encouraged the homeworking revolution, with subsidised places on business courses and similar programmes in addition to the backing for broadband. There has been official recognition for the part small home-based enterprises play in re-creating local economies, supporting shops and services, and reducing the need for new construction because one building fulfils two roles.

The current relationship between homeworking and country living has something of the chicken-and-egg question to it. Some people move to rural areas with a partner's job or for other personal reasons and have to explore the possibility of working from home because there is no employment locally to match their skill set and they are too far from the nearest city to make commuting an option. Others move to the countryside because they want to work from home and only by moving beyond the commuter zone can they afford a suitable property with enough space. They frequently make a social sacrifice in terms of leaving behind friends and an established lifestyle, but a new, less frenetic way of life is in most cases a part of the desire to work from home. With attaining a better work–life balance such a crucial motivation, there is no doubt that a disproportionate number of homeworking dreams come with roses around the door, but while it is possible to set up a successful home office in even the most remote corners of the UK, rural homeworking does bring its own challenges. As a general rule, the more isolated you are geographically, the further ahead you have to be able to see and plan.

>Does the technology reach that far?

Before you put in an offer on a house in the country, or make the decision to work from one you already own, you need to ask a few fundamental questions about the availability of communication technologies in the area.

▶ Which mobile phone networks have coverage?

Even if you can switch and keep your number, if you are expecting clients, suppliers and colleagues to visit you on business you need to consider whether you expect them to be incommunicado while visiting you.

▶ What broadband speed can you obtain?

Enter the postcode or landline number at www.broadbandchecker.co.uk to get location-specific information on the availability of ADSL, cable and satellite broadband and a round-up of the prices, deals and speeds offered by a range of providers. Bear in mind, though, that uploads tend to be slower than the advertised download speed, and that there has been much negative publicity about customers receiving speeds that are a fraction of those they are paying for. The best way to check is to run a test from the property using any one of the free commercial websites such as www.broadbandspeedchecker.co.uk and www.broadbandchoices.co.uk set up to do this.

▶ Is there Wi-Fi coverage?

Wireless technologies have acted as a lifeline for homeworkers and businesses in more remote stretches of the UK, including vast areas of northern Scotland, where providing ADSL still doesn't make economic sense. The UK is already the second biggest user of Wi-Fi in the world and the coverage is increasing all the time. In terms of the market, however, it is often focused on areas that already have ADSL, as a convenient alternative or for staying connected on the move.

▶ Are you in a 3G area?

As 3G is dictated by the location of mobile phone companies' masts, it is theoretically possible to live somewhere with no ADSL, cable or Wi-Fi service but still connect to the internet via 3G. In reality, however, this is unlikely, at least for the time being. The availability of 3G is increasing as the focus in innovation and improvement continues to be on mobile technology, but all the networks concentrated their 3G coverage on urban areas at first and catch-up in rural regions has been slow. Be wary of claims from networks that they cover a high percentage of the UK as the figures are almost certainly calculated by population rather than physical geography. Instead, ask to see an up-to-date coverage map in a shop or use the online postcode checkers offered by all the 3G networks. Some also show predicted future coverage.

So what if you are living in the country but seem to be off the radar as far as the communications providers are concerned? If the Wi-Fi internet connection in your area flits between low, very low and dropping out altogether, and you can only get enough mobile phone reception by leaning out of an upstairs window, you may be in a statistical minority but you are not alone.

That fact is important for two major reasons. Firstly, the nature of many small home businesses in rural areas means your clients are quite likely to be either local or based in equally remote locations. Experts in rural enterprise caution against the assumption that in this day and age everyone is permanently logged on to the internet, insisting that from a rural viewpoint the successful enterprises are those that are not based entirely on a virtual communication strategy, and businesses that are solely online are losing out on quite a lot of customers. As a homeworker with a job to do, you or your company may be willing to invest money in technology in a way that householders using it only for leisure simply won't. Having the inside track on the locality of your client base – and other important contacts – can be crucial in knowing whether an email, fax or old-fashioned letter will be quickest and most reliable in reaching them, and even something as simple as that they can be contacted only via a landline at certain times.

> **Definition:**
>
> ## Wi-MAX:
>
> Short for Worldwide Interoperability for Microwave Access, Wi-MAX is an in-the-pipeline alternative to Wi-Fi internet access that uses towers similar to mobile phone masts to give broad coverage rather than simply small hotspots. Already tested by BT in places such as Cornwall, Wales and Scotland, it is being seen specifically as a solution for isolated areas rather than a substitute where faster alternatives exist.

Secondly, other homeworkers in the vicinity are likely to be plagued by the same problems and there can be big benefits from joining forces. On the whole, it is too late to campaign for ADSL broadband, but the mobile phone companies offering 3G could be the next to respond to proof of market demand. And if Wi-Fi is also limited (and you could be waiting a very long time for Wi-MAX) then an expensive option like satellite broadband could become a possibility. You would still have to shoulder the significantly increased connection costs of £60-plus a month but the initial outlay on the equipment – currently upwards of £1,000 – could obviously be reduced to a tiny portion of that figure if split among a group.

>Meetings in the middle of nowhere

You are unlikely to be able to work successfully from home anywhere if your daily work schedule is packed with compulsory meetings, but even if such get-togethers are a less or are even a less frequent occurrence, they can prove a challenge if your base is more remote. If you are an employee with little jurisdiction over where and how meetings are held, there isn't much you can do beyond planning in advance for the time and expense of travelling to and from the office and perhaps – if

the timetable is fairly regular looking at spending only part of the week homeworking so you are close at hand when you have to be.

If, on the other hand, you are self-employed, running your own business or have a more influential position within the company, you can take a more proactive approach to finding alternatives to face-to-face meetings. What these are obviously depends on the purpose of the meeting, how many people are involved and the facilities available to them, but technology is making it easier and easier to trade information at all levels without having to leave your desk.

▶ **Telephone:** Many homeworkers point out that if you are stuck in an office all day, the temptation is to get out and have a meeting when often all you really need to do is talk. If it's only to be an infrequent event, you can conduct a conference call from any normal landline phone for a few pence a minute via any 'instant' conference call service provider.

▶ **VoIP:** Voice over Internet Protocol has long since lost most of the quality issues it struggled with in the early days, instead offering free or extremely cheap phone calls and conference calls with the chance to add a webcam, ideal for showing graphics and suchlike to remote colleagues for an immediate response.

▶ **Videoconferencing:** Personal video teleconference systems increasingly offer improved performance at lower prices, with the availability of freeware as part of chat programs opening it up, but quality is still restricted by broadband speed in some places. Hiring out a videoconferencing-equipped meeting room for an important presentation or meeting if facilities exist locally brings you as close as currently possible to being face to face.

▶ **Instant messaging:** Instant messaging is slowly being adopted professionally as well as socially and can be the most efficient way to make quick queries and requests of colleagues at another location.

▶ **VPN:** Virtual private networks allow distant colleagues to work together, accessing the same files without the security concerns of placing them on a public network like the internet. See Chapter 5 for more information on choosing the technology to suit your individual needs.

When only a face-to-face meeting will do, don't assume that you always have to do the travelling. Your boss and colleagues may not be impressed if you suggest they take a few hours out of their working day and enjoy the scenic route down to your place, and obviously you will always offer to meet clients wherever is most convenient to them, but you might be surprised at how keen they are to see your country set-up. Rural homeworkers in industries such as PR, marketing and design report that their clients love visiting, whether it's a lunch meeting in the local low-beamed pub or coffee in the kitchen, complete with muddy dog or cat. If they are homeworkers or aspiring homeworkers themselves – and the chances get greater all the time – then it gives a feeling of shared values, and even if not, they are at the very least pleased to discover that their fee isn't being inflated to cover the costs of an uber-stylish office or studio.

>Long-distance travel

If you will have to travel, whether for meetings, conferences, exhibitions or just in the normal course of your work, don't underestimate the additional time required for negotiating country lanes or using small railway branch lines. Do some trial runs if possible and stay aware of school holiday dates even if you don't have children as the influx of cars into and out of popular areas such as the West Country will have a huge impact on journey times.

With the public transport services in many rural areas infrequent or non-existent, you may be forced to take to the roads for business travel. Particularly if you have to make long journeys to major towns and cities, it could well be worth investigating car-sharing options – cutting the costs and easing any concerns you may have on an environmental front. Join or create a local car pool or look for someone going your way at websites such as www.nationalcarshare.co.uk, www.liftshare.org, www.mylifts.com or www.freewheelers.co.uk. On the plus side for rural transport, small regional airports usually require far less time for checking in and security, making flying a good option for some journeys with little wasted time involved.

From a financial perspective, using trains and planes for business travel calls for considerable forward planning. The cheapest seats on many routes sell out or are withdrawn from sale a month or more before departure, and advance booking can make the difference between public transport being very good value and expensive. If you are still discussing making the move to homeworking with your company, negotiate at this early stage what travel – including that to and from the office when it's required – you can legitimately claim as expenses. After all, it's no longer a routine commute and you now have other overheads associated with your home office. If you are self-employed or running a business, look very closely at what you can offset when you do your tax return.

>Where are the suppliers and services?

For anyone running a product-based business, the exact location of suppliers, distances to cover and modes of transport are crucial factors, but for other homeworkers the first thought of shops and services all too often comes only when the last ink cartridge is empty or the printer packs up mid-report. It is an inevitable fact that office supplies stores are distributed far more sparsely over less populated areas – and also often less likely to be open out of normal working hours. The solution for consumables such as paper and toner is probably to use the online shop of one of the major office superstores. Their prices tend to be lower because of the scale on which they are operating, thus counteracting any delivery charge, but it does mean you have to approach your stock-taking with military discipline so you're not caught out. With repairs and more specialist equipment, look locally first and ask around for recommendations. There is a growing number of small-scale businesses, part workshops and part shops, being run from private homes, many of them offering a knowledgeable, personal service with a cup of tea thrown in!

If your work calls for a lot of postal traffic, particularly if it is time-sensitive, reliable distribution could prove to be problematic. If you rely principally on normal Royal Mail services, work out the exact routes taken by the vans so you know where you can get the latest possible collection time. Despite high-profile opposition, the government is currently pushing ahead with plans to shut more than 2,500 post offices, mostly in rural areas. This follows closures over the past two decades at a rate of some 300 a year. While a few enterprising individuals have turned the situation into a business opportunity – a handful of pubs around the country now offer postal services with their pints – for the majority, it is more likely to cost money. It may not sound like a big deal to jump in the car to the nearest post office because the one in your village has closed, but when you are right up against a deadline, those extra minutes can be crucial and for someone running a home-based mail-order company, for example, the impact on cost and time is likely to be significant. Bear in mind, too, that a lot of courier firms will only accept long-distance or remote runs if you pay for both legs of the journey as they are unlikely to find another client on the same route.

>Overcoming professional isolation

Rural homeworkers, especially those who have made the move from a more urban environment and a busy office at the same time, often have a similar story to tell. The practical hitches are easy to overcome with a little bit of time and organisation, but despite all the benefits, there may be some sense of professional isolation.

This can be a psychological issue but can also have material ramifications. Anyone who has recently launched a business or set up as a freelancer has a brand to market and networking is vital. Similarly, pooling resources locally can be much cheaper and more effective than relying on expertise at the other end of the country. And while trading ideas via phone and email is valuable, it is hard to over-emphasise the benefits of getting away from the computer for a few hours, particularly in the all-consuming early stages.

The number of people moving out to the country after establishing a career in the city means that there are now more highly qualified, experienced professionals living and working in rural areas than ever before. Tapping into their knowledge and contacts while sharing your own can help with everything from the IT in your home office and your accounts if you have just turned self-employed to the website and publicity for a new business and even the photographs for your brochures. Unfortunately, there is no database of such networking groups and many of those that do meet regularly do so on an informal basis and not under the umbrella of any name or organisation. Again, word of mouth and local media are the best sources, though women can find details of WiRE (Women in Rural Enterprise) networks and links to other groups by region at www.wireuk.org. Social networking websites such as Facebook are also worth a look for activity in your area. Alternatively, set something up yourself – you'll probably be surprised at exactly who you have living within a couple of miles of your home.

You should check out the professional credentials of anyone you meet in this way before giving them your office or business details. Similarly, actually trading skills – legal advice for web design work, for example – can result in a lot of bitterness and even legal threats unless all involved are confident that what is being offered and received is equal in value. It often works better, if people don't mind taking their turn in the limelight, to have each member of a network give some form of presentation to everyone who might find their experience useful.

>Beware the community spirit

Part of the pleasure of switching the hustle of the city for village life is the much-talked-about sense of community. Of course country living is not all friendly neighbours, borrowed ladders and home-made cakes, but unless you are determined to cut yourself off from it entirely it is almost inevitable that you will end up on the committee for something (and being able to identify the owner of every car that comes down the road). Which is all very well and good – and, indeed, probably a large part of why you settled there in the first place – but there have been some cautionary tales from those who have fallen foul of informality in business. Keep a few basic principles in mind, whatever the social pressure, and don't let being part of the community leave you out of pocket.

> 'Starting this business was a huge challenge. Due to the remoteness of the house there is no telephone exchange to connect to'

- ▶ Most business is all about buying and selling – goods or services – at the right price. By all means reward loyalty with reductions but think twice before you offer a local discount per se. If it fits with your ethos or you are confident it will generate more work, set the figure, flag it up and don't allow yourself to be negotiated down by anyone.

- ▶ Offering sponsorship or prizes at local events can be a strong marketing tool, but do the sums and don't become the Yes Man or Woman for every cause and activity in the area.

- ▶ If you need something to be done, whether it's a one-off job or an ongoing contract, shop around outside the area as well as asking for a quote from the local suppliers. Allow for anything you might save in travel and transport costs but don't pay over the odds or compromise on quality through home loyalty.

- ▶ Never take shortcuts with paperwork. Draw up contracts for every agreement you enter into, rolling your eyes and citing red tape if necessary. Disputes over who said what rage for years and rack up huge bills in small claims courts.

▶ Look closely at Health & Safety laws if you agree to take anyone on for work experience or similar as a favour. Also seriously consider the damage they could do your reputation if they say the wrong thing on the phone or make a mistake on the computer before you assign them any tasks.

▶ Define some working hours and stick to them, even if it means ignoring the doorbell or domestic phone line. There is a tendency for people to disturb homeworkers with 'quick' demands on their time simply because they know they're in and there is a lingering belief that their work time is somehow less crucial than it would be in an office. See Chapter 6 for more time-management tips and strategies to create a routine and avoid distraction.

>Are there any financial incentives?

During the 1990s and early years of this century, there was an added motivation for home-based businesspeople and entrepreneurs to base themselves in rural regions of the UK. The government and regional development agencies ran several different subsidy and grant schemes in parallel, including the England Rural Development Programme 2000–2006, which approved more than 3,000 Rural Enterprise Scheme projects, supporting thousands of eligible businesses. That came to an end in 2006, but a new scheme, the Rural Development Programme for England 2007–2013 was launched at the beginning of 2008 with some crossover in its aims and the financial support offered. The focus has shifted though towards a broader public picture and only entrepreneurial businesses that can demonstrate wider benefits for the locality and region will have a chance of meeting the criteria.

The more specialist programmes dealing with the use of agricultural land or the provision of broadband access, for example, have in the main now also finished. Fundamentally, the availability of financial incentives for homeworkers in rural Britain is currently very low. Those that are available tend to be localised and specific to particular industries, but you can check the 'Grants and funding' section of the Department for Environment, Food and Rural Affairs (Defra) website (www.defra.gov.uk/funding) for up-to-date details.

> 'When I look up from my computer I can see right down the valley – miles of amazing, dramatic countryside'

It worked for me...

Annette, 37, nr Skipton

Annette has worked from home for two years. She says:

'I run my own small business from home high up on a Yorkshire moor. The house is off grid with no mains electricity and all power is generated using wind and water turbines and some solar energy. I don't even have the luxury of a landline telephone. Starting this business was a huge challenge. Due to the remoteness of the house there is no telephone exchange to connect to, which presented problems with getting communications installed, and as my company Luvit Jewellery is based on e-commerce this was critical. BT quoted the cost of installing a landline connection at £123,000 so that wasn't an option! There is no mobile phone signal either, but to overcome that a booster aerial was fitted to the roof so one mobile phone will work and acts as the business line.

By far the biggest problem has been an internet connection. Obviously for my e-commerce site I needed a good, reliable service, but it looked almost impossible at times. I spent 10 months looking into all the options and was still searching for a solution whilst the website was in build, which was extremely disconcerting. The answer finally was to use wireless broadband, connecting to a nearby community signal. The only downside was that the small electronic receiver mast, situated a 40-minute hike away across the moor, needed a power supply. This was provided initially using a truck battery but that discharged within three days, meaning a trip up the moor with the wheelbarrow and a replacement battery. However, research showed that we could power the mast using a small wind turbine and since fitting one of these my working week is much improved.'

It worked for me...

David, 31, Devon

David, has worked from home for a year. He says:

'My office is in a very small attic room at the top of our old terraced house and I can actually only stand upright at one end but it would take a lot to get me to give it up. When I look up from my computer I can see right down the valley – miles of amazing, dramatic countryside. I can't imagine there are many people in Britain with a view like that from their desk.

Everyone who works for my company is based at home, including the guy who set it up. There are six of us now and only one lives in a town. If we didn't have this set-up, I don't think it would be possible to work from my village – unless I retrained as a farrier! There are no offices nearby and the only other people I know working from home around here are writers who are self-employed and don't have clients to speak to every day. We use VoIP so we all have company numbers and we can hold conference calls for free. We also use a virtual private network.

As a PR firm, we specialise in rural businesses or those with country clientele, so our clients appreciate that we live what we're talking and understand the issues. A lot of them are also hot on the green agenda, so we communicate mainly by phone and email. When I do visit clients, though, the one thing I couldn't live without on the country lanes is SatNav.'

Resources:

Useful websites

▶ Commission for Rural Communities: www.ruralcommunities.gov.uk

▶ DEFRA: www.defra.gov.uk

▶ Natural England: www.naturalengland.org.uk

▶ Ruralnet: www.ruralnetuk.org

▶ Scottish Rural Property and Business Association: www.srpba.com

▶ WiRE: www.wireuk.org

Creating a green office

10

One of the many pleasures of working from home is the knowledge that you are doing your bit for the planet. Ditching the daily commute will wipe out a large stretch of your carbon footprint, and you can set your own standards when it comes to purchasing, recycling and energy use. Organisations from some of the UK's largest companies to the government have promoted homeworking as part of the environmental agenda – a potential solution to traffic congestion and emissions, at the very least.

It's an idea that is easy to buy into wholesale. After all, big corporate offices are full of humming technology that nobody ever bothers to switch off, plastic cups and waste paper, all topped off with acres of strip lighting glowing into the night. In surveys, nearly nine out of 10 workers have stated that they don't believe their employers are doing enough to minimise their impact on the environment. However, recent studies have indicated that homeworking might not be all that friendly to the planet either. In fact, research by a firm of independent consultants concluded that the average full-time homeworker produces 2.38 tonnes of carbon dioxide a year – nearly a third more than a typical office worker, who only churns out 1.68 tonnes. That discrepancy could actually outweigh the benefits of leaving the car at home every morning. The researchers put it down primarily to the extra heating and power used by homeworkers, particularly over the winter months. Electricity use is obviously shared in a communal office – from heating to printers and even the kettle – so for a worker who is home alone it can be considerably more costly, both in financial and environmental terms.

Though a clear warning against complacency, these figures are far from universal – or irreversible. Working from home certainly can be the greenest option – better for convenience, comfort and your conscience than a traditional office – but the message from the recent backlash is that you have to be proactive about making it so. There are simple steps, as well as more radical moves, that everyone can take when setting up and running a home office to keep its impact on the environment to a minimum.

>The green house

Being at home all day has a staggering effect on the amount of energy consumed. On top of the extra equipment plugged into the sockets in the office, there is substantially increased demand put on heating, lighting, hot water and kitchen equipment such as the microwave, toaster and kettle. Following the normal guidelines advised for all households therefore becomes more important. A hippo water-saver in the toilet cistern and remembering to boil only the water you need for each cup of tea may seem futile in the face of all that office technology but these are the things, experts insist, that allow individuals to make a real difference.

The National Energy Foundation's *Act on CO2* at Home suggestions range from free, instant fixes – a microwave uses far less electricity than a conventional oven; freezers should be kept packed full, even if it's with scrunched up paper; the seals on a fridge/freezer should be tight enough to hold a piece of paper securely – to those requiring a bit of time or money – fit a room thermostat; put aluminium foil behind radiators fitted to outside walls to reflect heat back into the house. See the full list at www.nef.org.uk.

For more detailed, tailored tips on domestic energy use, complete a Home Energy Check on the Government-backed Energy Saving Trust website (www.energysavingtrust.org.uk) or call 0800 512012 for a paper version. The website also features a database of recommended energy-saving products including household appliances and heating, lighting and insulation equipment.

Reassess your energy supplier at least once a year, not just for competitive pricing but also green credentials. There are specialist companies offering 100%

renewable power, while some household names also now have a clean electricity product available. Compare tariffs at www.greenelectricity.org.

>An eco-office

If you have the luxury of being able to plan an office from scratch, whether a purpose-built shed or extension or a garage or outbuilding conversion, the materials and expertise are now available to make it as environmentally sound as you wish. If you want to work in an eco-cabin with solar panels on the roof and a rainwater butt outside, it can certainly be done. Companies specialising in green buildings can put in alternative energy sources, and in some cases construct entirely from recycled or reclaimed parts. Where that isn't realistic, they can source locally other options, such as untreated timber from sustainable sources for the frame and untreated sheep's wool as insulation.

Employing a specialist on your project can be expensive, and environmentally friendly materials are typically more expensive than conventional, mass-produced alternatives, but according to the Royal Institution of Chartered Surveyors, there is a clear link between a building's green features and its market value. However, if the cost of a full-on eco-office is prohibitive, or the structure is already in place, there is still a lot that you can do to boost your environmental credentials. Maximise natural light wherever possible – consider installing skylights or even fitting glass in internal walls – and ensure all windows are double-glazed. Don't purchase floorboards, window frames or other fittings without investigating whether they can be found secondhand. Check out the chemicals and toxins in any glues, paints, fillers and other products before they are applied, and look at options such as removable carpet tiles that don't require any adhesive.

Choose office furniture with the environment in mind.

- ▶ Consider buying secondhand
- ▶ Try metal, specifically recycled aluminium or steel
- ▶ If you are opting for wood, go for European varieties such as pine and oak over tropical ones such as mahogany
- ▶ Seek out more unusual materials from green retailers, such as bamboo, which grows very quickly, requires no pesticides and is biodegradable, wheatboard, which is made from harvest waste, or even recycled games console casings

▶ Watch out for foam cushions made with HCFC (hydrochlorofluorocarbons) – foams made with isoprene, acetone and even carbon dioxide are better

▶ Ask the manufacturer about VOC (volatile organic compounds) emission levels in furniture glues, foam cushions and carpeting – VOCs contribute to 'sick building syndrome', polluting inside air and causing headaches and other symptoms.

To minimise energy use, office furniture should obviously be positioned to benefit from natural light, and away from radiators to avoid blocking the heat circulation.

Remember indoor plants when adding the final touches to your home office Choose a species with a large overall leaf surface, such as a variety of *Ficus*, for maximum effect, and it will boost oxygen levels in the room, remove pollutants, reduce air temperatures and raise humidity. NASA research into the purifying properties of plants discovered that just one potted plant per 100sq ft (30sq m)of floor space can help clean the air in the average home.

>Choosing non-harmful equipment

Considering that the average PC pumps out 610kg of carbon dioxide a year, it is disappointingly difficult to ascertain the environmental impact of the technology you are buying. There is no universal symbol or ratings system such as exist in other product sectors, so for the moment the onus is on the consumer to do the research. Organisations such as Greenpeace (www.greenpeace.org/electronics) and Ethical Consumer (www.ethicalcomsumer.org) have devised their own criteria and produce ranking tables of the major technology brands with explanations of their current advantages and disadvantages, and their commitment to improved practices in future. Greenpeace's quarterly reports focus on a company's policy and practice on use of hazardous chemicals in manufacture and take-back and recycling once the product is obsolete. Ethical Consumer additionally takes into account other environmental factors, politics and the producer's human rights and animal welfare record. The Ethical Company Organisation (www.ethical-company-organisation.org) also runs an independent accreditation scheme and an online shopping programme at www.gooshing.co.uk, which includes both an ethical product rating and a price search facility across hundreds of internet retailers.

When looking to buy ethical technology, you need to consider three stages in the life of the product.

1. The manufacturing process

▶ Are any of the materials used already recycled?
▶ Are efforts being made to omit blacklisted chemicals such as BFRs (brominated flame retardants) and PVC (polyvinyl chloride)?
▶ Where are the machines made and what are the implications in terms of human rights and transportation?

2. Day-to-day use

▶ How much energy does the machine consume during normal use and in standby mode?
▶ What inbuilt options are there for keeping it powered-down when not in active use?
▶ What's the ethical story behind related consumables such as ink cartridges?
▶ Will upgrades be available to prolong the life of the equipment?

3. Disposal

▶ What proportion can be dismantled and recycled?
▶ Does the manufacturer or importer make it clear that the product will be taken back free of charge when you have finished with it?
▶ What will then be done with the parts?

There are a number of voluntary schemes setting standards in some or all of these areas, but while signing up to such a programme might be a step in the right direction for technology companies, it can carry more suggestion than substance for consumers. Criteria vary too widely to make comparison meaningful, and greenwashing is a growing problem adding to the confusion, with some brands too keen to emblazon their packaging with eco-symbols regardless of their relevance. Likewise, the lack of approval from a respected programme such as Energy Star or Electronic Products Environmental Assesment Tool (EPEAT) shouldn't necessarily evoke suspicion.

At the same time, there are an increasing number of niche independent green companies entering the technology sector. One UK-based firm recently launched a fanless PC system using just 15 watts of power; the same as a low-energy light bulb. While such innovations are impressive, the equipment obviously comes without the long-term global reputation of the big brands, and may not always offer the same capabilities and back-up when it comes to technical functions. Your individual requirements, and those of your business, will dictate which is most important if there is a compromise to be made.

> **Definition:**
>
> ## Greenwashing:
>
> Making misleading claims about the eco-credentials of products or services in order to present a positive public image and tap into the green market. One knock-on effect is 'greenhushing', whereby companies with legitimate environmental practices keep quiet to avoid being tarred with the same brush.

Likewise, downgrading your specifications before you buy will save both money and energy if your business needs don't require cutting-edge technology. If the hours you spend in front of a computer screen are minimal, bear in mind that laptops use as little as 50% of the energy of desktops (though, experts calculate that the amount of waste matter generated in the production of a single laptop can be almost 4,000 times its weight on your lap). Does the nature of your work justify a laser printer? If the speed and quality of laser isn't strictly necessary, inkjet or dot-matrix printers use up to 95% and 75% less energy, respectively. Are you working with images, designs and other visuals on screen, or just viewing basic word-processing and spreadsheet packages? The greenest option is a low-resolution, monochrome or crystal liquid display monitor.

One of the major areas of concern for environmentalists has been the disposal of office technology at the end of its working life. UK households throw away a million tonnes of electronic and electrical equipment a year, from kitchen white goods to computers, and e-waste is the fastest growing form of rubbish in the EU. The WEEE (Waste Electrical and Electronic Equipment) Directive came into force on 1 July 2007 and makes it a legal responsibility for shops to either take back your old equipment in store when you buy like for like (regardless of where the original was purchased) or direct you to the nearest drop-off point, which they will be helping to fund. They can charge for collection if you require it, but not for dealing with the obsolete products. The WEEE regulations have been introduced to tackle

What's in a label?

Have you noticed how many brands of paper, in particular, come in green (subliminal message: eco-friendly) and white (clean) packaging? Of course for some companies with poor environmental records it's the equivalent of selling eggs from factory-farmed chickens in boxes emblazoned with images of sunny cornfields. The government has introduced a Green Claims Code to help tackle the problem of deliberate and inadvertent greenwashing, but warns that manufacturers and retailers can invent their own claims and symbols, and images of globes, trees and flowers – along with statements such as 'environmentally friendly' – are meaningless unless backed up with facts or relevant accreditation from a recognised source.

Office technology

The European Eco-label (www.ec.europa.eu/environment/ecolabel), represented by the flower symbol, was established to be the definitive mark of approval for non-food products. They must be independently certified and meet strict criteria for all the main environmental impacts throughout their life cycle. However, despite the fact that the Eco-label covers 24 categories including personal and portable computers, in the UK there are currently no computing models making the grade.

Some products may carry logos bestowed by other national or regional schemes, such as the Nordic Swan in Scandinavia and Germany's Blue Angel. See the Global Ecolabelling Network at www.gen.gr.jp for details of foreign programmes and their criteria.

The Energy Saving Recommended logo (see www.est.org.uk/recommended), awarded by the UK's Energy Saving Trust, endorses some of the most energy-efficient products on the market across a wide range of sectors including office technology.

The Energy Star is an American system launched by the US Environmental Protection Agency (www.energystar.gov) and used on a voluntary basis within the EU. It deals with power consumption in technological equipment, and its logo means that the appliance meets its criteria for low energy use in standby mode.

Another American programme, EPEAT (www.epeat.net), was created by the Green Electronics Council to help consumers make greener choices when buying computing equipment. It evaluates products according to 28 efficiency and sustainability criteria.

Paper and other timber products

The most frequently used logo of all, the Mobius Loop, has no legal or formal authority. It can be used to imply that the product contains recycled material, or that it can itself be recycled after use. A not dissimilar icon with the word recycled is slightly less ambiguous, though again it is entirely voluntary and gives no indication of what proportion of the content it refers to.

At the very beginning of the life cycle the FSC (Forest Stewardship Council) tree logo (see www.fsc-uk.org) means that the wood used in the product comes from forests that have been properly managed according to strict environmental, social and economic standards.

Wood and paper products certified by the PEFC Council (Programme for the Endorsement of Forest Certification; www.pefc.org) have been independently audited as coming from sustainably managed forests.

More detailed information about recycled paper content can be found through the Papermaking Sector Body of the Confederation of Paper Industries' classification scheme (see www.paper.org.uk). This uses letters to denote the type of waste paper included: A = unused mill waste; B = unused printers' offcuts; C = white office waste; D = low quality waste. A classification of 75B/25D, for example, would then give the percentages used in the recycled paper.

The NAPM (National Association of Paper Merchants; www.napm.org.uk) Recycled logo is an assurance that the product contains a minimum of 75 % recycled paper or board.

The EMAS (Eco-Management and Audit Scheme; www.emas.org.uk) is a voluntary scheme that independently verifies a paper manufacturer's green credentials against stringent criteria.

the growing amount of electrical waste by setting recycling targets and making producers pay for treating and recycling old equipment. Under the new rules, for a consumer to throw old electrical goods away with the household rubbish is still not an offence, but the greener action if you aren't replacing it with a new purchase is to take it to the local recycling site yourself or call the council to request a pick-up. There may or may not be a charge for the service, depending on where you live.

>The paper trail

The green office products industry began with paper. It's come a long way since grey, grainy pads of recycled sheets first hit the shops – recycled paper now has its own quality spectrum with those at the higher end sufficient for almost every office task. You can source recycled envelopes, labels, folders, brochures and more, as well as printing paper. Do bear in mind, however, that unless it is specifically marked to the contrary, recycled paper is unlikely to be suitable for archiving purposes.

As with office technology, confusion reigns supreme when it comes to paper classification and accreditation, and greenwashing is commonplace. The best known of the recycling symbols, the instantly recognisable Mobius Loop, actually has no precise meaning and its use is entirely voluntary. See 'What's in a label?'.

All recycled papers are not equal. The amount of post-consumer waste included varies, as do the production systems and standards. Look for a respected environmental certification such as EMAS or ISO 14001. If companies are boasting other symbols, look into the exact criteria they have to meet – the much-used FSC tree logo, for example, relates only to responsible, sustainable forest management and has no bearing on what then happens to the timber. For paper containing virgin wood pulp, ensuring it is sourced from FSC-certified forests is a good foundation. It can be enlightening to look beyond the sustainability and recycling claims of some paper manufacturers and dig deeper into the cleaning and factory processes – there are now brands that use only biodegradable cleaners and chlorine-free bleaches for whitening paper

Choose the lowest acceptable weight of paper required for the task, and think ahead to disposal before purchasing large quantities. Check with your recycling contractor exactly what types of paper it will accept and how it needs to be sorted. Mixing up different types reduces the quality of the recycled fibre dramatically – the fibre yield for re-pulping and de-inking waste paper ranges from 60% to 92%.

>Environmentally friendly usage

With paper use, the principles are clear – get the recycling bin out, but only use it as the final stage in the process. Between 60% and 80% of the waste generated by offices is paper. Do you really need hard copies of email correspondence, reports, even accounts? Software packages have been developed specifically to allow people to access these documents on the computer far faster than they could dig them out of a file, and as long as everything is meticulously backed-up, there is no reason for such storage to be any less secure. Plus switching to digital filing might even give you space to move in the office – a single 100MB zip disk can store the contents of a four-drawer cabinet, while one CD-Rom holds nearly a room's worth of paper.

If you have to print, use both sides of every sheet of paper and select the draft setting to minimise ink use unless something higher quality is really required. Return empty toner or ink cartridges to the retailer for reuse if they operate a scheme, or alternatively donate them to a charity that does, such as Help the Aged or Action Aid, or arrange a collection by GreenAgenda (www.greenagenda.co.uk).

Buying eco-alternatives where they are available can make a significant difference – lighting accounts for 30% – 50% of the energy consumed in most buildings, but energy-saving light bulbs use 80% less energy that traditional bulbs. Do enable energy-saving features on all computers and copiers. Visit www.localcooling.com to download an application that will automatically optimise the power settings on a PC (a Mac version is in the pipeline), but remember that screen savers were invented to prevent phosphor 'burn in' on the screen and don't save energy.

The ultimate answer, however, right across the board, is to switch it off. Many office machines use almost as much energy on standby as they do when in use, with PCs the worst energy wasters. UK office equipment left on standby produces nearly 4,000 tonnes of unnecessary carbon dioxide every weekend, not to mention costing businesses more than half a million pounds in pointless energy bills. A photocopier left on standby overnight wastes enough energy to print 5,000 copies. There are now wireless gadgets on the market that can measure the electricity being consumed across your home via a sensor attached to the mains. The amount of power being consumed by each appliance when turned on, off or to standby – and the related cost – can be viewed at the press of a button.

>Your carbon footprint

Carbon footprints and related concepts such as food miles are a 21st-century obsession. Offsetting schemes with payments into clean energy projects, refore-station schemes and the like are hailed by some as saviours and derided by others as conscience-massaging gimmicks. If by working from home you have given up a daily drive to and from the office, one thing you can be sure of is that your personal footprint will have been significantly reduced. In addition, the new structure of your day may mean you now have time to walk the children to school, cycle to the gym, or take public transport to the supermarket.

However, if homeworking means you no longer have an office manager or purchasing department, some responsibility now rests on you for the carbon trail left by your incoming and outgoing deliveries. Perhaps you can source suppliers more locally. With forward planning, you might be able to avoid the use of couriers without compromising on the quality and service of your business.

Think about how far and frequently you are still travelling in the course of your work. Are face-to-face meetings with clients and colleagues essential or could at least some of them be replaced by teleconferencing? One survey of people regularly travelling by train for business revealed that nearly half of them would opt for videoconferencing as a preferable alternative, and experts have estimated that up to 35% of UK business travel could reasonably be replaced by teleconferencing.

>Better for business

Creating the greenest possible home office isn't just good for the environment and your scruples; it can also boost productivity and profits. The financial impact of energy-saving measures has been well documented, but there are other less immediately obvious benefits.

Worryingly, the air inside most homes and offices is up to 10 times more polluted that that outside. Toxic fumes ooze from most carpets, furniture, cleaning products, and office equipment; workers in buildings made of man-made materials are believed to inhale in excess of 300 contaminants every day. Green buildings designed specifically to improve air quality and lighting, incorporating cleaner technologies and materials, have been shown in studies to have a positive effect on workers' productivity and reduce the headaches, tiredness and nausea experienced.

On top of that, environmental awareness has proven marketing appeal. Consumers are increasingly checking out the eco-credentials of their suppliers, so if you are operating on a freelance basis or running a small business from home, you can expect to be asked by potential clients what measures you have in place. With more knowledge, and cynicism, than ever before, customers are looking for something more substantial than a token nod towards going green. More than 90% of people questioned in a recent poll expressed concern for the environment, with 55% stating that they want more information from businesses on what they are doing to address climate change. More than half even declared they would pay up to 10% more for products if they could be sure they were environmentally friendly.

> 'I actually worked out my carbon footprint before and after I started working from home using an online calculator and the difference was quite inspiring'

It worked for me...

Amy, 33, South London

Amy has worked from her home office for three years. She says:

'I'm no eco-warrior, but being at home all day has made me focus on being greener. I take more pride in the house and am more aware of making it a clean, healthy environment. I only use natural, chemical-free cleaning products because I'm actually there to breathe them in, and now I get through so much paper in my office I'm much stricter about recycling in general. There are energy-saving light bulbs in every room, and I've got really into green gadgets – I have batteries that are recharged by plugging them into the USB port on my computer, and I used a little solar-powered fan right through the summer because the room I use as my office is small and gets quite stuffy.

I do have to pay a little bit more for some things but I've also made some small savings. I now reuse all the large envelopes and Jiffy bags I get sent because I bought some stickers that go over the address and have a green message printed on them – mine say 'Save trees, use these' and 'How many times can you reuse this packaging?' I didn't want to look like a cheapskate, particularly as the mail is going out to the people who pay me, but I think these are fun and portray me in quite a good light.

I actually worked out my carbon footprint before and after I started working from home using an online calculator and the difference was quite inspiring. That's even considering that I commuted by train, though if I left the office late I often had to get a taxi to the station and another one home at this end. I buy far more locally – everything from food to printer cartridges – and I walk to the gym and the shops, which I never had time for before. I was so worried that I would never leave the house when I started working from home that I bought a pedometer and set myself a target of 10,000 steps a day. That's actually quite a long way – about 5 miles – so it's made me fitter and greener as well.'

Resources:

Useful websites
Information and advice

- ▶ Act on CO2: www.actonco2.direct.gov.uk
- ▶ Better Business Guide: Guide to Energy Saving: www.thecarbontrust.co.uk
- ▶ Energy Saving Trust: www.energysavingtrust.org.uk
- ▶ Green Guide for Offices: www.lsx.org.uk
- ▶ National Energy Foundation: www.nef.org.uk
- ▶ Sustainable Office Forum: www.tsof.org.uk

Consumer guides

- ▶ Ethical Company Organisation: www.ethical-company-organisation.org
- ▶ Ethical Consumer: www.ethicalconsumer.org
- ▶ Green Consumer Guide: www.greenconsumerguide.com
- ▶ Green Electricity: www.greenelectricity.org
- ▶ Greenpeace: www.greenpeace.org/electronics

Further reading

- ▶ *Green Up!* by Will Anderson (Green Books)

No-nonsense A–Z guide to making your home eco-friendly, aimed at those without any DIY knowledge or skills.

- ▶ *Green Living for Dummies* by Michael Grosvenor and Liz Barclay (Wiley)

Simple strategies for reducing energy waste, ethical shopping and other steps you can take at home and in the office.

- ▶ *Change the World 9 to 5* (www.wearewhatwedo.org)

50 feel-good everyday actions anyone can take, wherever they work.

Rules and regulations

11

Think Health & Safety and the first images that spring to mind are hotel inspectors à la *Fawlty Towers* or the kind of gruesome industrial accidents involving giant vats or mincing machines that make the newspapers. Neither of which seem very relevant to anyone working at a desk in the safety of their own home. However, a surprising amount of the government's Health & Safety legislation does apply to homeworkers, whether employed, self-employed or running their own business. If you work for a company, some responsibilities lie with you and others with your employers – but have they ever seen or even questioned you about your homeworking arrangements? While many regulations pertaining to work premises and facilities don't apply in the home environment, there are certain clauses that do, and can be easily overlooked. Did you know that even if you work alone for yourself in your own house, an appropriately stocked first-aid box is necessary under Health & Safety rules?

And that's after you have informed all the necessary bodies about your intention to work from home in the first place. The quantity of red tape involved before you start working at home can seem off-putting, but in reality it is only where your circumstances or the scale of your home-based business are unusual that any obstacles are likely to arise. Deciding not to bother with the official channels, however, can prove costly. Don't put those phone calls and forms down the to-do list even when you are busy establishing your company, as, at the very least, there is usually a fine to pay if you are late registering your business interests. If planning permission is refused when your new office is almost finished, or there is a fire, flooding or a break-in before you have told your insurance provider about the change of use, the financial repercussions could be catastrophic.

Does anyone have a legal right to work from home?

The short answer is no. However, in certain circumstances employees do have a right to request flexible working (whether that means homeworking or part-time hours, or takes another form) and employers have a legal duty to consider such requests seriously and only reject them for good business reasons. This law applies to parents with a child under six or a disabled child under 18, and also, since April 2007, to carers of adults. The government has since announced its intention to extend the right to request further, to parents of older children, with the cut-off age still under review. Visit www.berr.gov.uk to keep abreast of reforms.

There is an interactive tool at www.direct.gov.uk to help you find out if you have the statutory right to apply for flexible working, choose the type of working that best suits your circumstances and prepare a case to convince your employer. Alternatively, the Advisory, Conciliation and Arbitration Service (Acas) provides free, impartial and confidential advice on all employment rights issues. Log on to www.acas.org.uk or call the helpline on 08457 474747.

Bear in mind that homeworkers are entitled to exactly the same rest breaks, sick pay, holiday and other leave (such as maternity or paternity) as anyone working in a conventional office.

>Are you allowed to work from your home?

The first thing to check is whether you have at any time signed a contract stipulating that homeworking is not allowed in your house, flat or block. This is most likely if you live in some form of social housing, but can also be a problem if you rent privately and even if you bought your home if, as is common in London, you don't actually own the freehold. The paperwork you have may give details of an official request or appeals process, but where it is an individual landlord or freeholder, as opposed to a corporation, who put in the clause, a direct approach can prove very successful. In these cases it has generally been added to the contract to protect them from the possible negative effects of a business operation on the premises, and the resulting complaints from other tenants and residents. If you have the necessary documentation to show that your homeworking won't mean increased noise and traffic, extra use of parking spaces and delivery lorries blocking the pavement, anecdotal evidence suggests there is unlikely to be a problem. It might actually be seen as an advantage to neighbours having somebody around during the day.

Whether you should inform your mortgage provider that you are working from home is something of a grey area. You will almost certainly have been asked the question on your original mortgage application forms and most experts do recommend that you inform the company so they can update their records. This won't actually impact on you, however, unless any alterations you are making change the building's nature from a residential home to commercial premises.

The same principle applies when it comes to your local authority. Planning permission is required for a material change of use even if no physical alteration is made to a building. Installing a workbench in your garage for domestic use is obviously your prerogative, but if you then use it for commercial purposes, you will probably need planning permission. There are no hard and fast rules and it can only be decided by talking to the local council, but if the answer to any of the following questions is yes, the likelihood is that an official application will be called for:

▶ Will the nature of the work you do from home lead to more people visiting the house and/or more traffic on the road?
▶ Will it mean your home is no longer used mainly as a private residence?
▶ Are the activities involved unusual for a residential area?
▶ Is there a risk that your work will generate unreasonable noise, smells or dust that could disturb neighbours, particularly outside of normal working hours?

Even if you believe your case is borderline or probably not subject to planning permission, it can be worth having the relevant conversations at this stage. It will mean you are already on the council's system or have the right paperwork to hand if a suspicious neighbour reports you further down the line, saving the time and stress of an investigation.

The kind of homeworking set-up that requires planning permission is also more likely to attract business rates. They can apply if you have people coming to the house on a regular basis for business, if you put up a sign outside or even if you simply have a space in your house, whether it's an upstairs room or the garage, that is dedicated to work. The last category might sound like it applies to most homeworkers, but the room has to be wholly commercial to be eligible for business rates, so if it doubles up as an occasional guest bedroom, living area etc., you'll only have to pay council tax as before. Ratings officers estimate that for 99% of homeworkers business rates don't apply, but if there is any doubt you should verify with the council or the local Valuation Office that you are not one of the exceptions. Find contact details for your area at www.mybusinessrates.gov.uk. There are sample situations with the assessment given at www.voa.gov.uk/council_tax/examples_working_from_home.htm.

If business rates are payable, the Valuation Office will come up with a rateable value for the areas of the house you are using for work. You may have a reduced council tax charge as a result. The business rates you will pay vary considerably, with the nature of your business, the location and size of your property and how you intend to use it all taken into account. Small Business Rate Relief can also reduce the cost by up to 50% so it's well worth investigating whether you could be eligible. There is a tool for estimating your rates bill as well as more information about rate relief at www.mybusinessrates.gov.uk.

One additional thing you should be aware of is that any portion of your house liable to business rates will probably lose its exemption from capital gains tax when you come to sell the property. There are ways to defer this so if you are planning a move, have a look at the government website at www.hmrc.gov.uk/cgt for details.

>Is your new office breaking the law?

If you are physically altering your property in order to create your home office, you will need to look again at the issue of planning permission, as well as Building Regulations approval. Building Regulations apply to building work in England and Wales and set standards for design and construction with health, safety and energy conservation in mind. If you are intending to convert the loft into your workspace, for example, you usually won't need planning permission unless you are going to extend the roof, and even then only in some circumstances. You will, however, be required to meet Building Regulations concerning the strength and stability of the structure including the new floor and existing roof, the safety of the stairway and escape in the event of a fire, and sound insulation from below.

Similarly, a garage conversion is unlikely to call for planning permission if it won't increase in volume, though it is particularly important to check if the property is in a conservation area, on a new housing development, or a listed building (in which case Listed Building Consent may be required; www.planning-applications.co.uk has some useful details). It will, though, usually be subject to Building Regulations covering ventilation, drainage and electrics as well as the walls, roof, flooring and the filling-in of the old garage doorway.

Contravening Building Regulations can lead to fines of several thousand pounds for whoever did the building work, and an enforcement notice from the local authority requiring the property owner to alter or remove work that doesn't comply. If this isn't done, the local authority can undertake the work itself and recover the costs. It is worthwhile to always be aware of the requirements yourself, but in the vast majority of cases if you are paying contractors to do the conversion or other building work for you, they will take responsibility for ensuring it is in line with Building Regulations.

Similarly, if you are having a new building erected, such as a purpose-built garden office, reputable companies should incorporate all the necessary steps for Building Regulations approval at design stage. More often than not, structures of this nature don't require planning permission, but the chances are that you will have to put in an application if:

▶ Your property is in a conservation area or a designated area of outstanding natural beauty, or it is listed.

▶ The building is less than 5m from your house.

▶ It will be more than 4m high.

▶ It will cover more than half of your garden.

▶ It won't solely be for your private use.

▶ The chosen site is closer to a public right of way than your house is, particularly if it is within 20m.

Again, if you are employing a specialist company, representatives should be able to advise you in detail on your individual circumstances, but it is wise to err on the side of caution from the start. If a retrospective planning application is refused, you will have to put everything back to its original state – and probably have to pay for someone to dismantle your office. The government's free booklet, *Planning: A Guide for Householders*, has more information and can be downloaded from www.communities.gov.uk/publications/planningandbuilding/planning-guide.

>Who else do you need to inform?

There have been cases of homeworkers putting in an insurance claim after theft or flooding, only to find that the household policy they have been paying the premium on for years doesn't cover any of their essential – and expensive – office equipment, or has been rendered totally invalid by the fact that they have been working from home. Most insurance companies now offer a tailored package specifically for homeworkers, or it is usually possible to apply an extension to a normal household policy to cover it. Check that the company you are considering using is a member of the Association of British Insurers at www.abi.org.uk, or find the best personalised deal via a registered insurance broker at www.iib-uk.com or www.biba.org.uk.

If your move to homeworking coincides with becoming self-employed or starting your own business, there are additional requirements and regulations you will have to address. The first step is to register with HM Revenue & Customs. If you don't do this within the first three months of working for yourself, you face a fine of £100. You can get more information and fill in the necessary form online at www.hmrc.gov.uk/selfemployed. For details of other legal obligations pertaining to setting up a business or as a sole trader, check out www.businesslink.gov.uk, www.startups.co.uk and www.hmrc.gov.uk/startingup.

>Health & Safety for homeworkers

It might be tempting to write the Health & Safety thing off as an irrelevant bureaucratic exercise, but when you consider that some three-quarters of all reported cases of work-related illness each year are musculoskeletal disorders such as back problems, or stress, depression or anxiety – things inherent in ordinary offices – then taking a few steps to lower the risk can seem relevant. The message from the Health & Safety Executive (HSE) is that you don't have to be handling hazardous chemicals or operating heavy machinery to benefit from having some kind of Health & Safety framework in place. Even if it's just a regular reminder that sitting in front of a computer all day with the phone wedged between your ear and shoulder leads to neck and back problems.

Whose responsibility?

You may assume that when you are working in your own home, hazards such as trailing computer cables and too much time spent staring at a screen are your responsibility, but that isn't always true. If you are an employee then your employers have to take steps to ensure your working environment and use of equipment are safe, even if you are based at home. The criteria they have to meet aren't as detailed or technical as those for premises they provide and maintain, which include rules on room volume per occupant, temperature, ventilation, cleanliness, maintenance records on equipment, and availability of drinking water and toilet facilities. However, they should at the very least offer training, information and any other necessary support for working safely with computers and other equipment required for your job at home. In return, you as the employee have a legal responsibility to take care of your Health & Safety and cooperate with the company policy and measures.

If you are self employed, you are responsible for arranging your own safety training and health checks where needed, first-aid arrangements and for organising sensible breaks during working hours. The definition of self-employed for Health & Safety purposes, though, can differ from that for tax purposes, so it is worth double-checking your status. If you run a home-based business, the legal requirements are the same as for a self-employed homeworker unless you also have employees. If you employ anyone, even on a part-time or temporary basis, you must have employers' liability insurance. This is what will cover compensation to workers who have been injured or made ill on your premises or under your responsibility, and your legal representation if you are prosecuted by the HSE or local authority.

Risk assessment and patterns

If you are running a business with responsibility for others then under the law you have to carry out a risk assessment to help you focus on the potential hazards in your workplace. Tools are available that allow you to do this yourself, including ready-made self-assessment forms that will ensure you have asked all the right

Demographically the UK league table for work-related illness, calculated by the average number of days lost per worker, currently looks like this:

1. East Midlands
2. North east
3. North west
4. Yorkshire and the Humber
5. Scotland
6. Wales
7. South west
8. London
9. East
10. South east
11. West Midlands

The occupations ranked from most likely to lead to work-related illness, according to the latest estimated average rates, are:

1. Protective service occupations
2. Health/social welfare associate professions
3. Teaching/research professions
4. Business/public service professions
5. Customer service occupations
6. Business/public service associate professions
7. Managers/proprietors – agriculture/services
8. Skilled construction/building trades
9. Health professionals
10. Caring personal service occupations
11. Skilled agricultural trades
12. Corporate managers
13. Transport/mobile machine drivers & operatives
14. Science/technical professions
15. Elementary trades/plant/storage
16. Science/technical associate professions
17. Culture/media/sports occupations
18. Textiles/printing/other skilled trades
19. Leisure/other personal service occupations
20. Administration occupations
21. Process, plant & machine operatives
22. Skilled metal/electrical trades
23. Secretarial & related occupations
24. Sales occupations
25. Elementary administration & service occupations

questions on websites including www.hse.gov.uk and www.safestartup.org. Even if you don't have a legal obligation to complete a risk assessment, this can be a useful process to highlight possible problems or precautions for your own home office.

VDU use

Apart from the universal risk of trips and slips, the most common areas for concern in small desk-based businesses are extended visual display unit (VDU) use and work-related stress (WRS). The incidence of headaches and eyes train has grown along with the integration of computers into daily working life, and the following regulations apply to employers where workers use VDUs as a significant part of their normal work, whether in a traditional office or at home:

▶ Workers must have breaks or changes of activity, and ideally have some discretion over when to take them. Their length and regularity, however, is not specified.

▶ Eye tests by an optometrist or doctor must be provided and paid for if requested. But the company is only obliged to pick up the bill for an employee's glasses if special ones are needed and normal ones can't be used.

▶ Training and information must be provided on how to avoid problems as a result of VDU use, and also on the steps the company is taking to combat them. Sample advice leaflets (also useful for self-employed homeworkers and those running one-man businesses) can be downloaded from www.hse.gov.uk

Work-related stress (WRS)

The European Agency for Safety and Health at Work has estimated that around a third of employees in the EU have WRS – caused when they feel that can't cope with what is being demanded of them. Employers have a legal duty of care to ensure their employees are not harmed by WRS, whether or not they work from home. Some of the resources produced for companies can also prove valuable for individuals with responsibility for their own wellbeing. Check out the 'Stress' section of the Institution of Occupational Safety and Health's Occupational Health Toolkit at www.ohtoolkit.co.uk, or the 'People, health and welfare' links at www.businesslink.gov.uk.

First aid

The minimum requirement for any workplace is an appropriately stocked first-aid box and someone appointed to look after that and other first-aid arrangements. This applies even if you are self-employed and working alone from home (in which case the appointed person is obviously you). Other measures such as first-aid training are only required if you employ a lot of people (more than 50 in a standard office) or work in a higher-risk industry. There is no legal list for what a first-aid kit should contain, but it should include various types and sizes of sterile dressing, bandages, safety pins and disposable gloves. A range of ready-stocked boxes that meet the guideline criteria are available on the market. If you spend a lot of time driving in the course of your work, you should have a personal first-aid kit in the vehicle.

Fire precautions

There are no legal requirements pertaining specifically to fire risk if you work alone from home, but your insurance policy may well be rendered invalid if you don't meet certain criteria laid out in the contract. Precautions are effectively the same as for normal domestic premises, though the extra electrical equipment in a home office can increase the risk. The Fire Protection Association offers a guideline checklist at www.fpa-fireriskassessment.com, which leads you through 51 questions to which you should be able to answer yes or not applicable. They cover such areas as:

▶ Is the upholstery of furniture in good condition?
▶ Is the fire alarm tested weekly?
▶ Are the fire extinguishers serviced annually by a competent company or person?

If the worst happens...

Since RIDDOR (Reporting of Injuries, Diseases and Dangerous Occurrences Regulations) came into force in 1996, any employer, self-employed worker or person in control of work premises has a legal responsibility to report certain dangerous or potentially dangerous incidents in the workplace. Only limited parts of the legislation apply to homeworkers without employees on their premises, and the likelihood of you ever having to act on it is very low, but it is important to know the letter of the law and how to report an incident, just in case.

If you are self-employed and suffer a major injury on your own premises, you or someone acting for you must provide a completed accident report form (F2508; available from www.riddor.gov.uk) within 10 days. You must also submit a completed disease form (F2508A) if a doctor informs you that you have a reportable work-related disease. See www.riddor.gov.uk for a full list, and also for details of exactly when you need to inform the authorities of other injuries or dangerous occurrences. If you are an employee, the onus is on your employer to report work-related accidents, injuries and diseases, so you must inform the relevant people at your company. If you do ever need to report an incident, it is a legal requirement to keep a record of the date and method of reporting, the date, time and place of the event, personal details of those involved, and a brief description of the accident or disease for three years after the occurrence.

'I also took the designs round to my closest neighbours and consulted them about how it would look from their garden'

Health & Safety: the facts and figures

▶ Over a third of major workplace injuries are caused by simple slipping or tripping.

▶ In 2006/07 2.2 million people in the UK had an illness they believed was caused or made worse by their work.

▶ Two-fifths of non-major injuries that require more than three days off work are caused by handling, lifting or carrying.

▶ In 2006/07 241 people were killed at work and 141,350 other injuries were reported under RIDDOR. Experts put the true number of reportable injuries at almost double that, at around the 274,000 mark.

▶ France has the highest work-related injury rate in western Europe. The UK has the third lowest, after Sweden and Ireland.

▶ The government's Revitalising Health & Safety target is to reduce the incidence rate of work-related ill health by 20% between 1999/2000 and 2009/10, but it is not currently on track to do this.

▶ In 2006/07, the HSE issued 8,099 enforcement notices, leading to 1,141 prosecutions and 848 convictions. The average penalty per conviction was £15,370, down to £8,723 if exceptional fines in excess of £100,000 are excluded. Many more cases were brought by local authorities.

It worked for me...

Jeremy, 45, Reading

Jeremy has worked from home for six years. He says:

'When I had my garden office built, the design and construction company made sure that all the dimensions were small enough that I didn't need planning permission. One of the ideas I initially had meant the roof would have been just over 4m at the highest point so they amended the plans so it squeezed under. They also suggested that I get an official letter from the council confirming that planning permission wasn't required so I had something to show the neighbours if anyone came knocking when the work started. That was good advice, and very easy to do, though I also took the designs round to my closest neighbours and consulted them about how it would look from their garden and whether there was anything they weren't happy with. I actually changed the colour of the roofing material and moved a window as a result, and it meant there was no real danger of complaints after the event.

My garden office is secure with locks on the door and windows, and the contents are covered on my household insurance policy though I do have to pay extra on my premiums. I have quite a lot of specialist technical equipment in there which is essential to my job so I've also taken out separate engineering insurance, which covers the effects of my computers breaking down, including reinstatement of data and any increased cost of working.'

Resources:

Useful websites
Planning advice

▶ Communities and local government: www.mybusinessrates.gov.uk

▶ Local council information: http://local.direct.gov.uk/mycouncil

▶ Planning Applications: www.planning-applications.co.uk

▶ Planning Portal: www.planningportal.gov.uk

▶ Valuation Office Agency: www.voa.gov.uk

Health & Safety information

▶ Business Link: www.businesslink.gov.uk

▶ Fire Protection Association: www.thefpa.co.uk

▶ Health & Safety Executive: www.hse.gov.uk

▶ Institution of Occupational Safety and Health: www.iosh.co.uk

▶ RIDDOR: www.riddor.gov.uk

▶ SafeStartup: www.safestartup.org

Further reading
▶ *How to get Planning Permission* by Roy Speer and Michael Dade (Stonepound Books)

A comprehensive guide designed to cut through the confusion over when permission is required and meet complex requirements for a successful application.

▶ *Essentials of Health & Safety at Work* (HSE)

One of the reference titles produced by the HSE, aimed at everyone rather than specifically management.

▶ *Pocket First Aid* (Dorling Kindersley)

Quick and easy-to-follow treatments and techniques authorised by the British Red Cross, St John Ambulance and St Andrew's Ambulance Association.

Reducing the costs 12

Setting up and running a home office can be an expensive business. By making a few cuts and compromises where it won't undermine your work or wellbeing, learning to take full advantage of the budget buys, special deals and tax breaks available, and linking up with others where there's savings in numbers, you'll find that homeworking leaves you not just healthier and happier but a little bit better off too.

>General finances

Get an accountant

If you are self-employed or running your own business, you will have to deal with a lot of accounting paperwork . Unless you have the time to read and understand all the small print and work out exactly how it can be applied to your situation, you are likely to end up paying too much tax. A qualified accountant will identify every last penny you can offset against your tax as a homeworker, whether it's a proportion of your rent, utilities bills or travel expenses. In most cases you will find the accountant's fee is outweighed – sometimes several times over – by the savings you can make.

Know your tax

Speak to your accountant or consult an officer at your local Citizens Advice Bureau to find out if there are any tax breaks or tax relief you might be eligible for (use the

search facility and get general tax information at www.adviceguide.org.uk). Or research what you are entitled to yourself via www. direct.gov.uk, www.taxcredits.inlandrevenue. gov.uk and www.businesslink.gov.uk. You could potentially qualify either through your personal circumstances – working tax credit for some parents and guardians, for example – or through the status of your business. Even if you are an employee, you might be missing out currently because, by and large, the onus is on you to claim.

Keep receipts

Hold onto the proof of everything you spend on work, whether it's for travel tickets, phone calls, newspapers and other reference materials or wining and dining clients. If you are an employee, you should be able to claim this money back as expenses from your company – you certainly shouldn't be out of pocket by choosing to work from home so arrange an urgent meeting to reassess the situation if you are. If you are self-employed or own a business, you can offset many of your expenses against your tax bill, including part of your home's running costs. Where many people found it was sufficient in the past to name a reasonable round-figure sum to cover this, HM Revenue & Customs now requires records to support any expense claim. You won't have to send bundles of receipts with your form, but it is important that you can prove specific expenditure if necessary. If you are dividing up household costs, you also need some evidence that the proportion you have apportioned to business use is justified.

Investigate grants

There are fewer grants and incentives than was the case a few years ago, but if you live in the right part of the country (typically in rural and deprived areas earmarked for regeneration), it is still possible you could get a helping hand financially. This is usually only true, however, if you are running a business and offering something back to the community, so it is the company rather than an employee who will benefit. Individuals might in some places get funding for further education or training to help their career or business. Contact your local or regional authority to find out about the situation in your area.

>Office furniture and products

Buy secondhand furniture

You don't have to buy new when it comes to office furniture. Chairs should be tested to ensure that the seat, lumbar support and arms are all still adjustable or you could be storing up back and other muscular problems, but an older desk may actually be a more natural fit with the style of the rest of your home, and you can often buy a full coordinating set-up in one go. Look for secondhand suppliers in the telephone directory, buy privately via local small advertisements, keep an eye out for notice of clearance sales at existing offices, or try specialist websites such as www.green-works.co.uk or www.freecycle.org. With the latter you won't have to pay a penny beyond your costs for collection.

Use what you already have

It sounds obvious, but do you really need a purpose built desk when you set out or would an old table do the job? Bedside cabinets can make really useful storage units with the added advantage that they are short enough to fit under your desk. And a coffee table may have enough surface area to take your printer or MFD, while open-topped crates underneath can function as drawers.

Double up

Don't take up room as well as cash by buying a dressing table for your guest bedroom if that's where your desk is going to be. Instead buy a throw in a shade that works with your colour scheme and go for an instant transformation when you have visitors.

Swap with friends and colleagues

Set up your own closed network in the Freecycle mould and the arrangements don't even have to be permanent. If you can borrow a desk until your neighbour's teenager wants it for college then it will at least prevent you having to pay for everything in one unmanageable lump sum – and lending your spare bed at the same time might just free up space in your home office too.

Register with the big companies

Register your details on the websites for office superstores and even supermarket chains – they'll often email you notice of sales and offers and even give exclusive online deals. Clearance stock, in particular, can have spectacular discounts. It is even worth dropping a line to manufacturers to ask if they have consumer panels and how they recruit people onto them. If you are lucky you can be sent products to trial and often keep in return for reviewing them on feedback forms or via a phone interview.

Get a loyalty card

When you have to make numerous repeat purchases of consumables such as paper and ink cartridges, the points you'll make on a loyalty card will quickly add up, allowing you to make some fairly substantial purchases for free over time. If possible, try to shop at office products stores that are part of a larger loyalty scheme rather than specific to one chain, and look carefully at ways to optimise your card's use – buying on triple-point days, for example.

Choose private-label brands

It is best to buy ink and toner cartridges specifically designed for the brand and model of printer or MFD you own, and a good ergonomic office chair is also worth investing in. With other products, though, particularly basics such as paper, as well as desks and storage units, don't assume that you have to be buying from the top end of the market. You will almost certainly find something to meet your needs among the store's own ranges, which are likely to be the cheapest available, and with some everyday essentials you can even undercut these by buying at the supermarket instead of a specialist shop. These won't necessarily be of any lower quality as the scale of production helps to keep the prices down.

Bulk buy where applicable

With space the most valuable commodity in many home offices, it is unlikely you are going to be able to store a year's worth of printing paper and other consumables. However, look at the catalogue for the office product superstores and you often find that buying just three of one item brings the price per unit down. You can even take advantage of offers aimed at larger offices if you can find other people within your local network who are keen to purchase a new desk, ergonomic chair, filing unit or even PC or other hardware at the same time as you.

>Technology and software

Buy a refurbished PC

There are undeniably deep pitfalls in buying a secondhand machine, particularly in a private sale. They may have the 'bonus' of software left on them (illegally), but you'll have next to no comeback if anything goes wrong. A refurbished computer, on the other hand, will have been cleaned and tested, and the companies that sell them usually offer some form of warranty. If you rely on a high-specification PC that will be in constant use, the potential problems of a used machine – combined with the speed at which technology is updated – may make secondhand hardware a false economy. If your use is relatively light and focused mainly on internet access and word processing, however, it may allow you time to save up for the right computer. Alternatively, looking at the secondhand market for a second machine should at least give you the opportunity to have a desktop as well as a laptop, or perhaps a second PC for family use so your work one can stay off-limits to the children.

Consider renting

If finding the capital for a new computer is an obstacle, or you are keen to upgrade or try new hardware but can't afford to take a risk on the unknown, renting might be the answer. You can find short or long-term leases for virtually every

PC on the market with regular payment plans so you can budget for it, and the possibly significant saving of free support if anything goes wrong with the machine.

Research free software

The majority of homeworkers don't have cutting-edge software requirements. Most need only word-processing, spreadsheet, internet and email packages and some anti-virus measures. But if bought new and directly from the makers, even this can be an outlay of several hundred pounds. If you are willing to forego the household names, however, you can pick up programs with much of the same functionality for nothing. The most secure source for such software is the Open Source Initiative, a non-profit organisation dedicated to providing software programs for download and use – free of charge. It offers the Firefox web browser and OpenOffice, which includes word processing, spreadsheet and presentation programs and allows users to create documents that are compatible with Microsoft Office. Visit www.openoffice.org for these free applications. There is a range of anti-spyware available to download without cost from the internet. However, be cautious when installing free software from other sites; ensure that it is what it claims to be and that it is legally available.

Build your own website

If you are keen to promote your services as a freelancer or business on the internet, you need to assess whether you need an expensive, professionally designed and maintained website at this stage. Some kind of web presence is all but essential these days, but if you are listed in the right directories that may be enough until you are more established and have more money available – and it will cost considerably less than your own website. Alternatively, create a homepage to lay claim to your domain name (which, incidentally, shouldn't cost you more than around £10, but is a classic area for the unknowing to be ripped off) and direct potential clients towards your email address and phone number for more information. You can even be more ambitious and add links with further details, tariffs and even a portfolio using a straightforward DIY website package or a deal that offers the necessary tools along with the domain name and related email accounts.

Sign up to an e-fax service

If your MFD does not come with an integral fax, buying one could be the expensive option. A growing number of companies are offering an e-fax service, whereby you are provided with a unique fax number to give out to clients and other contacts. Anything sent to that number is received by the company, which then scans and emails it directly to you. As a result, you can pick up faxes via your PDA, laptop or internet on your mobile while away from the office, and you don't have to worry about the initial outlay for a fax machine, or its maintenance, paper, ink and energy consumption, or the price of a dedicated second line. At well under £10 a month on average, the costs of an e-fax service compare favourably for the majority of people.

Don't print!

Following the advice of the green campaigners will also save you money and space. Invest in software specifically designed for digital filing and storage and aim to keep copies of everything on your computer system rather than your shelves. You can even scan in paperwork, though there may be legal reasons to hold onto original versions of some documents. Printers devour energy as well as pricey ink, toner and paper, so switching yours off as much as possible should have a positive impact on your bills as well as your shopping budget.

Opt for duplex printing

If you need to print regularly, you should ideally have a printer with a duplex function that will automatically reverse a sheet of paper and print on the other side too. It is obviously possible to reload used paper to do this manually but it's a time-consuming exercise. Halving your paper use can mean significant savings in the medium to long-term.

Change your automatic settings

You should ensure that the default modes on your computer and printer are set to power down after just a few minutes out of use. Otherwise you will be paying out unnecessarily on your electricity bill. And if the printer is turning out full-colour, high-quality or even standard copies when you only need monochrome drafts, you're wasting a lot of ink or toner too.

Back up online

Traditional methods of backing up ongoing work, accounts, databases and other essentials, such as external hard drives or CDs and DVDs, are very effective but can prove expensive, especially if they are outsourced. But there are companies offering online back-up services that can actually be free at introductory level and cost less than £5 a month even for a reasonably large-scale individual operation that is fully automatic and requires no input from you at all.

>Services and utilities

Use VoIP (Voice over Internet Protocol)

Why pay hefty phone bills if you can make your calls at a discounted rate or even for free over the internet? Most VoIP services offer a reduction of at least 30% on UK landline and mobile calls, and with some deals it can be significantly more. There is the cost of set-up and VoIP line rental but there are phone and broadband charges you will be paying already and it is very rare for a VoIP user not to make savings overall. Slight issues with the quality of the connection are still there on some calls, though they are now minimal and it's probably a compromise worth making. If you are an employee and the main office is also set up for VoIP then all your calls to colleagues will be free. Many providers offer a free trial so all you need is a broadband connection and a headset with a microphone to see if it works for you.

Don't pay for a business tariff

If you are a homeworker with a one-person operation, it is almost unfeasible that you will require the capabilities offered by a broadband deal or combined phone and internet package tailored to the needs of larger businesses. So you should register as a domestic user instead.

Choose a combined package

However good the individual deals, paying for separate landline and broadband or Wi-Fi services from different providers will nearly always work out more expensive than getting both from a single supplier. It's clearly a false economy if you end up with slow, unreliable internet access, though, so do research the reputation and records of the companies before signing up.

Pick the right plan

Most household telephone plans are chosen because they offer cheap calls during the evenings and weekends when people are in, but the pay-off is that they can be extremely expensive during working hours. As a homeworker, that will presumably be the period of peak usage for you, so look in detail at alternative packages. Calculate roughly what proportion of your calls are domestic, international, to a mobile or to a special-tariff number. If most are to landlines within the UK, there are packages available that offer unlimited calls to 01 and 02 numbers for a flat monthly fee, typically in the region of £10.

Say no to 0870

Companies often put forward their 0870 numbers, which can cost about 15p a minute to call, but they usually have cheaper alternatives behind the scenes. Use the independent website www.saynoto0870.com to find standard-rate 01 and 02 numbers as well as some free 0800 numbers.

Switch suppliers regularly

The recent proliferation of price comparison websites makes it easier and far less time-consuming to identify where the best deals on all your main utilities are to be found. If you are at home all day your water, electricity and gas bills will rise, so it is important to have the most economical plan. The markets are becoming more and more competitive and there are no longer huge differences in rates to take advantage of, but some companies do offer incentives to new customers so reassessing your suppliers on an annual basis can still pay dividends. Try www.uswitch.com, www.switchwithwhich.co.uk or www.moneysupermarket.com.

Go green

Put into practice the raft of energy-saving measures flagged up by eco-campaigners and, experts say, you could save up to £250 on your household energy bills. That figure is likely to be a lot higher for homeworkers, too, because office products such as PCs and printers are some of the greediest consumers around. Some of the measures do require initial outlay but others cost nothing – just turning off all your electrical appliances at the wall will make a difference as items left on standby account for 6% of your bill. See Chapter 10 for more ideas and information.

>Shared resources

Join a network

Try to find a group of like-minded homeworkers in your area. If none exists, try advertising for members and create one. You can then trade ideas and knowledge on everything from accounts, publicity, marketing and law to IT and web design – skills you might otherwise have paid a small fortune for.

Be part of a car-sharing scheme

If ditching the commute means you no longer need to run a car, look into joining a local pool that will give you access to a vehicle when you do have to make a journey by road. These work in various ways. You might be able to book a communal car for days you have a business trip to make, collecting it from and returning it to a shared garage. Or some schemes also try to unite people travelling in the same direction. Either way, you will usually only have to pay for the fuel that you use and your insurance as a driver, plus probably a small membership fee to cover maintenance and repairs.

Negotiate

Long phone or conference calls to international or even domestic clients might put a big dent in your homeworking budget, but to a large company the costs will be a drop in the ocean that are simply swallowed up. Try to arrange a system whereby they phone you rather than the other way round, or make it clear that you add the expenses for overseas calls or those over a certain value to your fees. Few big businesses will quibble with this if they are getting the service they are looking for.

>Longer-term investment

Create renewable energy

Working from home, especially if you are having construction or renovation work done to create your office, can be the perfect opportunity to look at installing one or more sources of renewable energy. This obviously requires a significant cash injection upfront but a ground source heat pump can save £400–£800 a year on heating bills and solar water heating can provide you with about a third of your hot water needs. Recent law changes mean you no longer need to go through a planning permission procedure to erect solar photovoltaic panels, which create electricity to run appliances and lighting. There are also government grants available in some circumstances to help with the costs of putting these renewable technologies in place. Contact your local Energy Saving Trust advice centre on 0800 512012 for further information.

Resources:

Useful websites

▶ Business Link: www.businesslink.gov.uk

▶ Energy Saving Trust: www.energysavingtrust.org.uk

▶ General government advice: www.direct.gov.uk

▶ HM Revenue & Customs: www.hmrc.gov.uk

▶ Money Saving Expert: www.moneysavingexpert.com

▶ This is Money: www.thisismoney.co.uk

Further reading

▶ *The Money Diet* by Martin Lewis (Random House)

Really practical money-saving techniques and strategies across all aspects of life from the man behind www.moneysavingexpert.com.

Trouble-shooting

13

>Technical problems

My computer has just packed up

If none of the usual measures have worked, for example rebooting, then it's time to call in the experts. If you can wait until normal working hours then the call-out fee will normally be considerably lower. IT support providers, like plumbers and electricians, have high emergency call-out rates over weekends, evenings and bank holidays. Some also calculate their charges on a mileage basis, so it can be worth searching for a local company.

Some companies offer telephone consultancy as a first port of call, and in a lot of cases that will be all you need. This is often only available if you are a client paying for ongoing maintenance and support services, however. Depending on the age and value of your computing equipment, how integral it is to your work and your own technical aptitude, paying for external IT help in this way can be a good decision. Look for companies that offer remote support, where their technicians can access and control your computer from their own offices, frequently saving the time and cost of a call-out.

My internet connection is very slow

This can be frustrating, especially when you are paying for a high speed service. Check the details of your contract with your internet service provider and whether you have a download limit. If so, your provider could actually be deliberately slowing down your connection speed because you are over your limit. Contact your provider to find out if this is the case – though they should email to tell you – and if your use hasn't been exceptional recently, you may have to look at upgrading to an unlimited broadband package. If it's a one-off, you can usually pay for the extra downloads per GB and have your speed restored.

Alternatively, the problem may be with the contention ratio offered by your provider – essentially, the number of people sharing your broadband connection. A ratio of 50:1 is normal, but some providers have much higher figures. If your connection is particularly slow at popular times of the day such as the evenings but fine at others then this is the most likely explanation. Unfortunately you will either need to reschedule your day to take advantage of off-peak times, or change your provider.

My printer is always running out of ink

Firstly, make sure your default settings are always draft quality and monochrome so you only use extra ink when you make a definite decision that you need or want it. Secondly, always ask yourself whether you really need to print before you hit the button. If you have a digital storage system for important documents on your computer (and backed up online or on CDs, DVDs or another hard drive kept elsewhere) you may not need to file a hard copy. Always switching the printer off after use will help reduce energy consumption and prevent you from simply using it automatically when it isn't necessary.

If you are already taking these measures, you may need to look at the printer you have chosen. Cheaper models especially are often designed to require replacement cartridges on a regular basis because it's on these consumables that the manufacturer makes a profit. There is the potential to at least save money on your frequent ink purchases if your printer is compatible for use with cartridges made by a third party and not just that specific brand, but be warned: these don't always provide the same quality of colour and durability, and some printer manufacturers may only value the warranty on the machine if it uses their own cartridges.

>Legal problems

My boss has turned down my request to work from home

The issue here is whether your employer has a sound business reason for the decision. Ask for some objective opinions from people who have a full understanding of the job you do within the company and its structure and operations. There are eight permitted reasons for refusing a request for flexible working from someone with a legal right to make one (the law is set to change on this so double-check that you are eligible at www.direct.gov.uk). The reasons are:

▶ Burden of additional costs
▶ Detrimental effect on ability to meet customer demand
▶ Inability to reorganise work among existing staff
▶ Inability to recruit additional staff
▶ Detrimental impact on quality
▶ Detrimental impact on performance
▶ Insufficiency of work during the periods you propose to work
▶ Planned structural changes.

Your employer must also explain the reason in relation to your individual proposal. If you still feel that the rejection is unjustified, you have 14 days from being given your employer's written reasons to lodge an appeal. Your appeal meeting should take place within the following 14 days, and you should be told whether or not your appeal has been upheld in another two weeks. Again your employer has to put this is writing with reasons.

At this stage you either have to accept the decision or put in an Employment Tribunal complaint. This can be done on only the following three grounds:

▶ The employer has not followed the procedure
▶ The employer has refused the application for a reason other than those listed above
▶ The employer's decision to refuse was based on incorrect facts

The tribunal can't force your employer to grant your request, only order that the decision is reconsidered. It can also award compensation of up to eight weeks' wages, currently capped at £2,320.

You are not entitled to complain simply because you disagree with the reason given, unless you are a woman and believe you have a valid indirect sex discrimination claim. If you win this, the compensation can be far greater but it is a serious accusation and you are unlikely to be able to rebuild a working relationship afterwards. But that shouldn't put you off fighting for your rights if your case meets the criteria. See the Equal Opportunities Commission website at www.eoc.org.uk or phone the advice line on 0845 601 5901 for more information.

Remember that as the employee you also have a set process to abide by, so don't risk being refused because you haven't followed the correct procedure. The easiest way to ensure everything is in place is to use the standard form available in the 'Employment Guidance' section at www.berr.gov.uk, but this isn't compulsory. See full details of how to apply on the same website. It is also worth considering a compromise option in advance. Perhaps another form of flexible working might help to fulfil some of the reasons you wanted to work from home.

My neighbours have put in a complaint about my new garden office

If you consulted your local council before beginning work on the office site, and either went through the whole planning application process or were officially told that you didn't need to, then there is nothing your neighbours can do. Show them the letter from the council to that effect if you got one at the time, or contact your council to ask for one now. The more informed you are about why your garden office is completely legitimate, the better able to convince your neighbours you will be, so get all the facts at your fingertips about its height, other dimensions, distance from your boundary and the public road and so on, as well as the legal requirements.

For the sake of harmonious relations, it may be worth asking your neighbours why they are unhappy and what measures you could take to appease them. For example, if they feel their garden is being overlooked, perhaps you could put up blinds on that side, or if they consider it to be an eyesore, you could stock up on hanging baskets and other large potted plants and flowers to place along the outside wall.

If you didn't consult the council before putting up your garden office, go back to the company you bought it from to double-check that they have ensured it meets all the relevant criteria. If there is any doubt, you may have to apply for retrospective planning permission. This should be considered without prejudice, exactly as it would have been had you submitted the application in advance. If permission is refused, though, you will probably be issued with an enforcement notice at the same time. This would almost certainly require you to take down the office and return your garden to its previous condition, and you will be given what the planning enforcement service considers a reasonable time frame in which to do this.

I'm moving house and unsure about the legal implications

If your home office in the old house wasn't classified as a commercial space, which means you paid council tax and no business rates, then your homeworking has no legal implications for the sale. If it was, then you will be liable for capital gains tax on the commercial portion of the property. For 2008/09 the proposed rate is 18%, with the annual exempt (tax-free) amount set at £9,600. The government is currently pushing through reforms on capital gains tax, so you should discuss your individual circumstances with your accountant to ensure you have an accurate, up-to-date picture.

With regard to your new property, you should probably inform your mortgage provider that you again intend to work from home, though whether you have to isn't clear. It's unlikely to have any impact unless you are planning to make dramatic changes to the property that will transform it into commercial premises. You will need to assess the new house for planning permission requirements and eligibility for business rates once you have decided where your home office will be and what alterations, if any, you will be making. See Chapter 11 for more details on the criteria.

>Financial problems

My old PC isn't coping but I can't afford the one I want

You could think about renting, at least as a short-term solution. Buying secondhand isn't recommended if you are looking for a high-spec machine for work use, so this may be the best option, particularly if you are undecided about exactly which model you want to upgrade to. You can try out new hardware to see if it meets all your business needs and personal preferences without having to find – and risk – a large upfront payment. Longer-term leases obviously work out better value, but either way you will have a regular payment plan that should help with budgeting. You also won't have the financial pressure of putting money aside for emergency maintenance and repairs because these should be covered under your hire agreement.

I seem to spend all my time doing admin and other routine tasks that were done by someone else in the office

Homeworkers do out of necessity become Jacks or Jills of all trades, taking control of everything from cleaning and IT to Health & Safety within their own office in addition to their main job. If you are an employee, ask your manager if there are any practical ways you can still plug into the support services in the main office. If you previously had help with typing up letters, entering information onto databases and similar tasks, that should continue. Your salary is based on the skills and experience you have for your designated job, and your employer will want to maximise the number of hours you spend doing that.

If you are self-employed, then the tasks that you outsource depend on your budget, needs and personal preferences. Most people prioritise paying for outside help in areas such as accounting, law and IT, which require specialist knowledge that they don't have themselves. Beyond that, though, if you do the calculations you may well find that with the amount of time admin is taking you away from running your business or fulfilling contracts, you can justify the cost of outsourcing it. There are several companies and (often homeworking) individuals offering virtual secretarial services so look around for someone who can meet your requirements, fit in with your hours and with whom you click – they are going to be handling a lot of your business documents so it's important that you trust them and feel they understand what you do. Ask yourself whether you are ever going to need to meet them face to face, because that will obviously restrict you geographically. You can search directories of virtual assistants by services and location at www .allianceofukvirtualassistants.org.uk.

I want to work from home but we're planning to start a family and I don't want to miss out on any maternity leave or benefits

If you continue as an employee, you have the same entitlements whether you are based at home or in the office. And if you are planning to submit a request to work from home after your maternity leave, then it can be useful for you and your employer to have had a trial run for at least six months and ironed out any problems. You have a legal right to time off work during pregnancy to attend scans and other necessary health checks, as well as ordinary sick leave where applicable, and you may well miss less work – and operate more productively – if you can take travelling out of the equation.

If the move to homeworking coincides with you becoming self-employed then your circumstances will change and, particularly if your employer offered a generous maternity package, you will probably lose out financially. Think really carefully about whether this is the right time to do this for you because it may mean you have to return to work more quickly after the birth too. If you do decide to go ahead, look closely at the dates involved as these can affect what you are entitled to. Maternity Allowance is paid by Jobcentre Plus for a maximum of 39 weeks while you are not working, at a weekly rate of £117.18 or 90% of your average gross weekly earning, whichever is smaller, but as a self-employed worker you are only eligible if you are registered as such with HM Revenue & Customs, have been self-employed for at least 26 weeks of the 66 weeks preceding your due date and earning an average of at least £30 a week in that period. The 26 weeks don't have to have been in a row. Find out more and download the relevant form at www.direct.gov.uk.

>Personal and health problems

I miss having other like-minded people to talk to about work

Consider joining a business network. Find one relevant to you via national bodies such as Women in Rural Enterprise (www.wireuk.org) or the Women in Business Network (www.wibn.co.uk), through industry organisations for your occupation or in local press. Most organise regular get-togethers, which are a chance to socialise as well as widen your circle of business contacts. If there is nothing in your area, it is relatively easy to get a group up and running. You don't need a venue unless you plan to have more structured meetings – just reserve a couple of tables at a pub or café and put up some posters or distribute fliers in the vicinity. You can also join online groups on social networking sites such as Facebook and chat and trade ideas with homeworkers in a similar situation at the other end of the country.

I feel a bit claustrophobic in my home office all day

Make sure you leave the house at least once a day, even if it's just for a brisk walk round the block. This is good for your body, which will suffer from sitting in one position for hours at a time, and will help avoid these feelings of cabin fever. If the nature of your work allows, take your laptop or notebook out to a park or quiet café once a week – your mind will benefit from the change of scene. Fresh air is hugely beneficial so open windows and if possible take the opportunity to work in the garden when the weather allows.

You can also try to make your workspace feel as light, fresh and airy as possible. Think about repainting the walls if they are too dark, remove any furniture that makes the room cluttered and gives it an oppressive feel, and invest in attractive lamps that give warm but effective lighting. See Chapter 3 and Chapter 4 for more suggestions on how to open out a small area and give the illusion of greater space.

I've been getting bad headaches since I started working from home

The most likely reason for such headaches is eye strain. Get your eyes tested to check whether you need glasses or contact lenses for VDU (visual display unit) use, but if you had no problems before you became a homeworker then the problem probably lies with your monitor and its positioning rather than your sight. Invest in an anti-glare shield for your screen and move the monitor to avoid glare from sunlight or overhead lighting. If you are short of options for siting your computer, switching off the ceiling lights and replacing them with freestanding and table lamps, as well as fitting blinds, may help.

Another possible cause of headaches is dehydration. Keep a bottle or jug on your desk so you refill your glass automatically, and limit your caffeine intake to three cups of tea or coffee a day and preferably fewer.

You should also check for poor ventilation in your home office as a potential cause, and act on any feelings of mounting stress, which can also have physical side effects such as headaches.

I can't get through to my friends that I'm not actually free during the day

This is a common problem, particularly if you have friends who aren't currently working, or who are at home with children during the day. The best course of action is generally to become uncontactable over working hours. If you have a separate business line, only give the number to work contacts. If not, make sure the phone in your office has a caller ID screen so you can let personal calls go through to voicemail. Ensure that your partner, children and anyone else who may need to get hold of you urgently have their own 'hotline', whether it's a second mobile phone or just their own individual ringtones so you know instantly when to pick up.

Set up a free email account if you don't already have one and use that for all your personal messages so that your business address remains exclusively for work. Only reply to private emails and phone messages after you have finished for the day.

>Environmental problems

I don't have kerbside recycling where I live

The Household Waste Recycling Act 2003 requires local authorities in England to have provided kerbside collections for everyone by 2010, though if you live in a block of flats, a very narrow street or a remote rural area the council may argue that it's expensive or difficult. In the meantime, you can recycle your office waste yourself. Take used paper to your nearest recycling site – find it using the postcode search at www.recyclenow.com. Empty ink or toner cartridges should be returned to the retailer or manufacturer if they operate a reuse policy. Otherwise some charities, including Help the Aged and Action Aid, can exchange exhausted peripherals for between 25p and £4. Just check that the make and model are acceptable. GreenAgenda (www.greenagenda.co.uk) runs a scheme to collect empty cartridges.

Items of office technology can be dropped off at the closest recycling site with provision for electrical appliances, or, under the terms of the EU's WEEE Directive, taken to the store where you are buying the new replacement, regardless of whether or not it is where you purchased the original. You can also request a collection from the shop or the council but there may be a charge for this service.

I don't own my house so I can't make any permanent changes to bring my heating bills down

Ask your landlord, if possible – tenants in this position often get permission for even quite major alterations because making a property more environmentally friendly is perceived as adding to its value. If you really can't, there are still many temporary or easily reversible measures that can make a significant difference to the energy consumed by your heating system.

▶ Look into fitting thermostats in each room or putting individual valves on radiators so you can heat only the areas of the house you are working in during the day.
▶ Place sheets of foil on the walls behind radiators to reflect heat back into the room.
▶ Adjust curtains so that they stop above radiators and don't block the warmth.
▶ Leave space between radiators and furniture, which will absorb heat and prevent it circulating in the room.
▶ If you have an open fire, buy a chimney balloon for when it's not in use. Up to 50% of heat can be lost up a chimney. Alternatively, you can get much the same results with scrunched up newspaper or even an old pillow, but don't forget it's there.

I don't have the money at the moment to make my home greener

There is plenty you can do for free or just a few pounds – see www.nef.org.uk and www.energysavingtrust.org.uk for ideas. But If you are looking at some more large scale adaptations, investigate whether you are eligible for any government grants or other financial assistance. The first important thing to realise is that you don't have to be on a low income or benefits to qualify – the majority of grants are available to any household in the UK.

The Energy Saving Trust runs the government's Low Carbon Buildings Programme on behalf of the Department for Business, Enterprise & Regulatory Reform. You can apply for a grant of up to £2,500 per property towards the cost of having approved microgeneration technologies put in by a certified installer, but you do have to prove that you are already minimising your energy requirements. Technologies covered by the scheme include solar photovoltaics (domestic solar panels for generating electricity), wind turbines, ground source heat pumps and bio-energy. See www.lowcarbonbuildings.org.uk for the criteria you need to meet, details of the process and the opportunity to apply online.

The government's long-term aim of cutting carbon emissions by 60% by 2050 has also been passed down to UK energy suppliers, who have targets under the Energy Efficiency Commitment. In order to meet these, they now provide a range of offers that significantly reduce the cost of installing energy-saving and renewable measures. These are open to everyone, regardless of whether or not you have an account with the supplier, so shop around.

Local authorities also have a number of grants and offers available within their own areas. To see what assistance you might be entitled to on the basis of your personal means, location and the type of home you live in, use the online search tool at www.energysavingtrust.org.uk/gid.

>Other common problems

I'm worried that having all this technology at home is an invitation to thieves

The best place to work is often right next to a window where you get plenty of natural light without glare and an inspiring view, but depending on the layout of your home this may also mean your computer and other equipment is on display. First and foremost, double-check that your insurance policy covers all your office equipment, then take preventive measures. Install a household alarm system if you think it is warranted, or buy a sturdy cable-and-fixing-plate lock for your PC and MFD or printer. These have the advantage of being quite highly visible so should act as a deterrent to anyone attracted by the machines on view. You could also consider buying theft recovery software, which should allow experts to trace your PC or laptop if you are the victim of a burglary.

Everyone in the house can hear my confidential work calls

If this is a real issue in your house and you have a dedicated room for your home office, you could look at having it professionally soundproofed. There is a huge range of materials on the market to lie under the carpet, line the walls, and even insulate the door, ceiling and windows. This is obviously an expensive measure, however, and the cost is probably only justified if there are other people in the property most or all of the time and you are being continually distracted by household and outside noise as well as being overheard.

Other solutions requiring significant money and effort to implement are replacing windows with double or even triple glazing, and hanging a solid external door instead of a standard interior-style one, which will have a hollow core. You should also fit seals around the door. As a general rule, acoustic experts recommend that at least 25% of your office should have a soft surface, such as carpet, wall coverings, curtains or upholstered furniture, to absorb sound.

If the problem is only occasional, you could try a white noise machine or CD. It obviously won't cut down on noise but will mask sounds, including your telephone conversations. Sound conditioners use sounds from nature and are intended to be soothing as well as practical. Psychologists often use them to block sound from other offices.

Clients won't take me seriously because I'm home-based

Attitudes are changing and you might be pleasantly surprised by their reaction, but if you truly believe that being known to work from home will have a detrimental effect on your business, you don't have to tell your clients. Join a club with meeting facilities – both formal

and social – in a convenient local location and use that for all your face-to-face encounters. Add your business name into your home address, or even set up a PO box if you are not happy with that, though they can be inconvenient. Have professional business cards printed with a dedicated landline and mobile number so there's no risk of other family members answering the phone. Buying a domain name so that your email address contains the name of your business rather than a free provider will also give you clout.

Index